T0353913

Nadiya's Simple Spices

NADIYA HUSSAIN

For Nani, our pomegranate.
It all started at home with you.
Long may it continue.
For generations and generations.
And generations

Nadiya's Simple Spices

Curries and more from
Nadiya's home kitchen

Photography by Chris Terry

Introduction 6-15

Break-feast
16-37

Noon
38-63

Staples
64-85

Middle of the table
86-115

CONTENTS

Veg at the table
116–151

Stuff on the sides
152–183

Sweet stuff
184–205

Tea, biscuits and relax
206–229

Index 230

Thanks 238

INTRODUCTION

Growing up in my world, we ate rice and curry, twice a day, seven days a week, all year round. We knew nothing else. And why would we want to? Wholesome meals, cooked from scratch, every single day. My fellow Lutonians across the other side of town may well have been eating pies, cake or pasta, but we were simply having curry. It was familiar, it was habitual and it was home.

But this was a habit I broke almost as soon as I left home and had my own children. As I straddled two worlds, so did my palate. I was exploring, dipping into a world that was more than rice and curry. There was so much I hadn't smelled, explored, tasted or experienced. And there was so much to learn and, most importantly, eat.

After years of experimenting and eating absolutely everything from all cuisines, there has been a switch in recent years in what my family loves to eat. As my children grow from being kids to teenagers, close to adulthood, our curiosity has led us right back to the beginning, right where I started. Grateful for all we have tried, tasted and experienced, our hearts and stomachs turned out to lie in home cooking, just the way I remember it: rice, curry and all the beautiful colours of the traditional Bangladeshi kitchen where I was raised.

So when I ask, 'What would you like for dinner?' the response is almost always the same. 'Curry,' or 'Something with rice,' which my long-deceased grandad, who used to be a rice farmer, would have been very happy about indeed.

Nothing has been more thrilling than sharing my family's food with you over the years and now that we're back where I started, I want to take you on this part of my food journey too. This book is packed with the recipes I grew up eating. Some are original to the core, while others have been adapted to fit with where I am in my life now. But what hasn't changed is the flavour, the vibrancy and the joy this food brings. So, join me and my family through these pages and eat with us.

The Core of This Book

Often when people think about cooking with spices, I believe there is a notion that there will be hundreds of spices, huge ingredient lists and prep work that can go into the double digits of hours. Well, you're not wrong, it can absolutely be like that. So now you're probably thinking, well, this book sounds like a lead balloon! What is she trying to say?

Life, special occasions, celebrations and, in my family's case, the arrival of unannounced relatives meant growing up it could be exactly that commotion. Mayhem like you've never seen; ingredients that spilt off the kitchen table and onto the floor; hours and hours of cooking - day into night and then back into day. All of which ultimately resulted in delicious vats of food, overfed bellies and exhausted cooks.

But at its core, the cooking I grew up with was delicious but simple. We almost always used only a few spices - whole and ground. These were mixed in various combinations and used at different stages of cooking to create a unique flavour every time. Like the rest of my family, I have these exact same spices in my home today. The same spices my mum uses now, the same spices my Nani used before her and, no doubt, my Great-Nani before her too.

So, no, it's not complicated - it never was - and I want to share these eight spices with you. You can then truly experience the ease and simplicity of cooking delicious food using just these spices you have at home.

Four whole spices

1. **Cardamom pods**
2. **Cinnamon sticks**
3. **Bay leaves**
4. **Fennel seeds**

Four ground spices

5. **Ground turmeric**
6. **Chilli powder**
7. **Ground cumin**
8. **Curry powder**

There is a secret ninth spice too, using - yes, you guessed right - the eight spices I just told you about. That's my very special Art Masala, which simply means 'eight-spice mix'.

And that is it. Eight spices are all you need to create any recipe in this book - from breakfast all the way through to dessert. Enjoy the simplest way to cook extraordinary things with confidence.

1
4
2
5
7
6
3
8
Art Masala
(eight-spice mix)

The Eight Spices

Four whole spices

BAY LEAVES

Native to the Mediterranean but also found growing in gardens all over the world, are evergreen Bay trees and shrubs that produce dark green leaves, perfectly aromatic and essential for infusing in soups, stocks, stews, sauces, fish, rice, potatoes and so much more. Use them fresh or dried – just remember that fresh will be more pungent. Smelling of sweet balsamic, nutmeg, a hint of cracked black pepper, pine, citrus and vanilla, Bay will add a subtle layer of beautiful flavour to your meals. Slow cooking them is key to coaxing out the true depth of taste, so make sure your dried leaves are less than a year old to make the most of their flavour.

CARDAMOM PODS

From South Asia and shaped like miniature rugby balls, cardamom pods are packed with tiny dark seeds that are warming, lemony, minty, fragrant hits of versatile flavour. You can add them whole or crushed to elevate your curries, rice, sauces, soups, sweet pastries and even your tea. Known as the Queen of Spices, cardamom is related to the ginger family, which may explain why it has such a distinctive flavour. It supports healthy digestion too.

CINNAMON STICKS

Dalchini, also known as cinnamon sticks, are wonderfully aromatic spirals of bark that come from the cinnamon tree native to Sri Lanka, India and Myanmar. There are two types of cinnamon: Ceylon, which is light and sweet, and Cassia, which is spicier and from China, Indonesia and Vietnam. Both offer rich, warming and earthy tones. These deep golden quills offer a depth of flavour to both sweet and savoury meals, everything from Korma to cakes.

FENNEL SEEDS

Zesty, sweet, warming and licoricey, fennel seeds come from the flower of the fennel plant and will give your meals a delicate and earthy taste. Looking almost like cumin seeds, fennel seeds are small and rectangular in shape with pale green ridges. Perfect for baking, hearty stews, soups, fresh spring salads, rice, noodles, curries and tea, fennel will melt into the background of your cooking to form a strong, deep base.

Four ground spices

CHILLI POWDER
Distinctively fiery and ranging from vibrant orange to a hot red in colour, chilli powder is a spice not to be underestimated – even in its milder forms. Sprinkle into sauces, your favourite curries, pakoras, bhajis, samosas and more, for an injection of spicy, hot, fruity flavour. Remember to add a little at a time so you can let the chilli flavour fully develop for a full preview of how your meal will taste.

GROUND TURMERIC
Rich sunshine yellow, turmeric is as delicious as it is nourishing, not least for its anti-inflammatory properties. If I'm ever feeling under the weather, I'll make sure I add turmeric to my ingredients list. Peppery, gingery and earthy, add generous pinches of turmeric to soups, dressings, tofu, lentils, curries, into boiling rice water and even hot and cold drinks.

GROUND CUMIN
A familiar favourite, this spice instantly brings depth and warmth to every meal. Stirred through buttery rice, or rubbed onto a cauliflower before roasting, onto lamb or pan-fried with beans or chickpeas, cumin's aromatic, savoury, nutty, citrus flavour transforms your raw ingredients. Essential in Tikka Masala and almost all Indian curries, cumin – also known as Jeera – is best known for its ability to bring out hidden depths of flavour.

CURRY POWDER
This is a power spice to have in your spice box as it is a mixture of savoury: cumin, turmeric, ginger, garlic, mustard seeds, fennel, bay; and sweet elements: cinnamon and clove. The amount of black pepper determines how spicy it is, and sometimes chilli is added too. Slow cook your curry powder so that all of the flavours have time to develop. Add it to roasted vegetables, soups, sauces and of course curries for a deep, warming taste.

This book is all about using eight spices in different ways. With just these spices you can make every recipe in the book. Everyone needs to have a good masala mix in their repertoire, so I want to share my art masala mix, which you can use in lots of the recipes. When trying to source the spices at the supermarket, don't forget to make your way to the Asian/World Foods aisle too. It's a treasure trove of goodies and inspiration!

Art Masala (eight-spice mix)

Makes about 550g spice mix

28g cardamom pods
3g bay leaves
34g fennel seeds
100g cumin seeds or ground cumin
38g ground cinnamon
100g ground turmeric
44g chilli powder
200g curry powder

Start by using a spice grinder, which is the best tool for the job. Lots of smoothie-makers also come with a milling blade that works well to really crush down these whole spices. Put the cardamom pods in the grinder, husk and all. (Imagine trying to de-pod that many – you would have given up before you'd even started. I know I would have.) Whack them in and blend to a fine powder, then pour out into a large bowl.

Now put your bay leaves, fennel and cumin seeds into the same grinder and blitz to a powder. If your grinder is small, you can do each spice alone, but just note that when doing the bay leaves, always blend them with the fennel seeds. They need the seeds to get them moving enough to crush to a powder. Add to the bowl. Mix thoroughly, being sure to do this after each addition as it's important to make sure that the mix is well blended.

Now for the cinnamon. I prefer to use ground cinnamon as it's readily available and will save you from having to crush something quite hard – why should we if we don't need to? Add to the bowl and mix.

Chuck in the ground turmeric and mix. Add the chilli powder and mix. Lastly, add the curry powder and give everything a good stir.

That's it. Now you have your very own ninth spice, using ingredients you already have at home. Transfer into a jar or jars and you are ready to go!

+ Dried spices can last for a very long time – just be sure to store them in a cupboard that is dark and out of direct sunlight. If you have spices that have sat for a long time and you want to rejuvenate them, add what you need to a non-stick pan over a low heat and gently toast. This will release the oils and restore the spices as if they had been freshly ground today.

Nadiya's six foolproof steps to perfect rice

1. MEASURE YOUR RICE

The easy way to measure your rice is in a mug. The average coffee mug is 280g of rice which will feed a family of four as an accompaniment. Multiply up and down to suit the number of people you are cooking for.

2. NEVER FORGET TO WASH YOUR RICE

Always wash your rice with cold water till the water runs completely clear. Rice is very starchy and this is what makes it gluey in texture. Washing your rice helps take away the starch. To wash the rice, place it into a bowl or saucepan and cover it in water. Use your hand to move the rice around and watch as the water becomes cloudy. Drain and repeat until the water runs clear.

3. CHOOSE YOUR PAN WISELY

Always cook your rice in a roomy pan, so the rice has space to move when boiling. This means that each grain has room to cook thoroughly and evenly.

4. HOW MUCH WATER?

Once the drained rice is in the pan, add cold water so the water is just 2cm above the level of the rice. This will work no matter how much rice you are cooking.

5. BOIL

Put your rice on a high heat. Be sure to stay close-by and stir the rice to encourage movement or the bottom layer will stick to the base and you will get burnt rice. Move the rice until it starts to boil, which is when the rice will be already moving itself.

6. AND FINALLY, STEAM

Once all the liquid has been absorbed, turn the heat down to the lowest it can go, pop the lid on and leave to steam for 15 minutes, for fluffy, light, delicious rice.

Break-feast

It was a treat in Bangladesh when you had a loaf for breakfast, or 'loof' as everyone liked to call it. It was sweet, buttery and pillowy soft, very unlike the bread we have with our beans and eggs. So, this is my version – slightly sweet and very delicately aromatic from the turmeric. Instead of butter, I'm using ghee. Wait till you see the bold yellow colour – it's a loaf like you have never seen before.

Bangladeshi Breakfast Loaf

serves

Prep: 20–25 minutes. (+ proving)

Cook: 45 minutes (+ cooling)

- 350g strong bread flour, plus a little extra for dusting
- 7g fast-action yeast
- 7g fine salt
- 20g caster sugar
- 1 teaspoon ground turmeric
- 4 medium eggs, plus an egg yolk for brushing the loaf
- 50ml whole milk
- 115g ghee, softened
- oil, for greasing

To serve

salted butter

Start by putting the strong bread flour into the mixing bowl of a freestanding mixer. Add the fast-action yeast to one side of the bowl and the fine salt to the other.

Now add the caster sugar along with the ground turmeric and give everything a good mix till well combined. Make a well in the centre.

Crack your eggs into a jug and whisk till you have an even egg mixture. Pour in the whole milk just until you have exactly 250ml of liquid. You may need more or less than 50ml, but that is why it's best to do this part in a jug.

Pour the wet mixture into the well in the centre of the dry mixture and mix everything using the dough hook attachment on your mixer till you have a roughly mixed dough.

Now turn up the speed and begin kneading till you have something that resembles a smoother dough. Start adding small knobs of the ghee, allowing it just to incorporate before adding another. Do this till you have finished all the ghee.

Keep kneading for 6 minutes on a high speed till you have a dough that is smooth and stretchy. Transfer the dough to a bowl, cover and leave in the fridge for 2 hours.

Have a 900g loaf tin greased and lined ready for the dough.

Tip the dough out onto a floured surface. Knead a few times and shape it so it neatly fits into the tin. Pop into the tin, cover and leave in the fridge overnight so you can make fresh bread first thing!

When you are ready to bake, preheat the oven to 180°C fan.

→

Take the dough out of the fridge, uncover and brush all over with the yolk for a beautiful shine. Bake for 15 minutes. Reduce the oven temperature to 150°C and bake for another 30 minutes.

Once baked, leave in the tin for 10 minutes and then remove from the tin, get rid of the paper, and leave to cool completely on a wire rack.

This is best eaten toasted dry in a pan, like my Nani does, till golden on both sides, with lashings of butter. You can also just toast in a toaster, but I highly recommend my nani's way. I can confirm it's the best!

+ When you are making something like this that requires a few hours of waiting, I would highly recommend doubling the recipe up. The second loaf, wrapped in foil, will freeze well, so you can have a second loaf without the wait.

This is bread pudding like you've never tried before – at least not the kind I know of, as a Brit. My version is really easy and why wouldn't you want to have pudding for breakfast? Cocoa sweet, with the scent of fennel and crunch of hazelnut, it's like the famous chocolate spread but fancier.

Chocolate Bread Pudding

serves

4

Prep: 10 minutes

Cook: 10–15 minutes

For the bread pudding

2 teaspoons fennel seeds

1 litre whole milk

3 tablespoons cocoa powder

5 slices of white bread, torn into chunks

3 tablespoons butter

50g caster sugar

To serve

chocolate hazelnut spread

seedless raspberry jam

100g roasted chopped hazelnuts

Take a medium non-stick pan and add the fennel seeds. Toast the seeds over a medium heat till you can smell the aroma.

Tip out into a pestle and mortar and crush to a fine powder. Now add back into the pan along with the milk. Bring the milk to the boil and then turn the heat down to a gentle simmer.

Add the cocoa powder and mix through, then add the white bread in chunks and, while simmering, use a whisk to break down the bread. Keep whisking till you are left with a smoother mixture. Add the butter and keep whisking till the mixture comes together, then add the caster sugar and mix through.

Serve the bread pudding in bowls with dollops of the hazelnut spread and jam and then sprinkle over the chopped hazelnuts. Enjoy!

+ If you ever have any leftover bread, or have a loaf that needs to be used up before going away, pop it into the freezer, sliced. It can be toasted from frozen and even be used in this recipe.

Parathas were always a bit of a treat. Whenever we would go dress shopping, we would stop off and pick up parathas midway to sustain the never-ending day of looking through reams and reams of fabrics, dresses and saris. You can make a paratha with pretty much any type of filling, though it's usually savoury. So, with that in mind, I have come up with a paratha that isn't savoury – yes, it's sweet, filled with a frangipane mixture inside its puff-pastry exterior. It is all the things I love, and I don't have to go dress shopping to enjoy it!

Frangipane Almond Parathas

makes

Prep: 12 minutes
Cook: 24 minutes

2 x 500g blocks of puff pastry, defrosted and chilled
200g ground almonds
2 teaspoons almond extract
2 teaspoons ground cinnamon
2 medium eggs
70g caster sugar

To serve
icing sugar

Unwrap the blocks of puff pastry and cut each block into four equal squares, then pop on a tray and set aside.

Take your ground almonds and scatter into a non-stick frying pan in an even layer. Pop over a medium to high heat and toast the almonds, making sure to keep them moving by stirring and toasting till a light golden colour. This should only take a few minutes.

Take the pan off the heat and scrape the almonds into a bowl. Add the almond extract and ground cinnamon. Stir and leave to cool to room temperature, which should only take a few minutes.

Now add the eggs and caster sugar and mix through till you have a paste that is thick and can be formed into a ball. Bring the ball together and, using a knife, cut into eight equal wedges.

Take a square of puff pastry and, using your hands, flatten the dough so you make space for the filling. Add the filling to the centre and use the excess dough around the edges to encase that filling.

Dust the surface of the worktop with flour and place the dough ball seam-side down. Roll the dough ball to a 21cm circle.

Pop the non-stick frying pan back on the hob over a medium to high heat. Place the paratha in and dry-fry for 2 minutes on each side. Do the same to all eight.

To serve, dust (when I say dust, I mean shower!) with icing sugar, tear, share and enjoy!

+ If you are making these and don't want to eat them all at once, you can get to the rolling stage and lay them one on top of the other, with sheets of baking paper in between, and freeze. To cook, you simply take away the paper and dry-fry from frozen for 4 minutes on each side over a low to medium heat.

This is a classic dish eaten during the months of Ramadhan when we fast. It's a great way to fill up and replenish any lost salt and is buttery enough to keep you warm all day in winter. I, however, have not restricted myself to a particular month to eat this – we eat it all year round. It's quick, it's simple and it's delicious. This is the ultimate salty meets sweet!

Ginger Butter Rice

serves

4

Prep: 10 minutes
Cook: 45 minutes (+ cooling)

For the rice
100g basmati rice
750ml cold water
½ teaspoon salt
40g ginger, peeled and grated
100g unsalted butter

For the maple sauce
50g linseeds
100ml light maple syrup

To serve
chopped dates

Start by adding the basmati rice to the pan with the cold water. Add the salt along with the ginger, put the pan over a high heat and allow the whole mixture to come up to the boil, stirring occasionally to stop the rice from settling and sticking to the base.

Once it has boiled, the rice should be bloated and now we need to break it up gently. Lower to a medium heat and whisk continuously for up to 30 minutes until the rice has broken up.

To get a smooth mixture, add the butter and keep whisking till the butter has melted and emulsified. You should end up with a beautifully rich buttery mixture that is perfectly cooked.

Take off the heat and leave to cool and thicken a little more. It will be ready to eat soon, I promise.

Add the linseeds to a medium non-stick pan and toast till golden. They don't change colour massively, but you will be able to smell the nuttiness. Take off the heat, add the maple syrup and mix together.

Serve a bowl of the ginger rice with a sprinkling of chopped dates and a good drizzle of the maple sauce.

+ This is such a versatile recipe. If you wanted to eat it as a savoury soup, you can add 150g of shredded chicken at the end of the cooking process to make a gorgeously simple chicken soup.

Hot spicy potatoes for breakfast is the kind of meal we had every day when we were out in Bangladesh. It was hearty and after a long morning of work on the fields, it gave you that energy and second wind to get back out there. I didn't do the work in the fields, though I often watched, but I never failed to join them for this breakfast. My version is made with hash browns, which are quick and easy and save a load of time. Simply spiced, they are squished into buttered floury baps with a runny egg.

Hash Smash Breakfast

serves

4

Prep: 5 minutes
Cook: 15 minutes

4 tablespoons vegetable oil
3 teaspoons curry powder
1 teaspoon salt
150g spring onions, thinly sliced
500g hash browns, defrosted
4 medium eggs

To serve
4 large floury baps
butter, to spread
ketchup

Start with a high-sided, medium non-stick frying pan that has a lid. Pop onto the hob over a medium to high heat, add the vegetable oil and as soon as the oil is hot, add the curry powder and salt and mix very quickly.

Promptly follow with the spring onions and cook till they are softened and have taken on some colour.

Add the hash browns and, using your mixing spoon, break up so they toast in places to create a crunch. Nothing needs cooking here, simply reheating.

Make sure the hash browns are in an even layer in the pan, then crack in the eggs in four different places, creating your four portions.

Turn the heat up, pop the lid on and cook the eggs to your liking. I like them runny and this only takes a few minutes. As the eggs cook, the potato base should get crispy. Meanwhile, split and butter the baps.

Take your buttered bap and a portion of your smashed hash and eggs and get it right into the bap. Add a squirt of ketchup, top with the bap. Now you are ready to smash this breakfast!

+ Don't be limited to hash browns where this recipe is concerned. You can use leftover roast potatoes, chips from last night's take-away, potato waffles or cauliflower hash browns – the list is endless!

Yoghurt is a big part of the culture I grew up in. Something that we can buy off the shelf in Britain without a thought was a treat in Bangladesh. Served mostly at weddings, we could not wait for a wedding to eat yoghurt. This recipe starts off with shop-bought yoghurt, sweetened and flavoured and served with the most refreshing frozen minty grapes.

Mint Grapes with Yoghurt

serves

Prep: 12 minutes (+ freezing)

For the yoghurt
100g pecans
500g full-fat Greek yoghurt
3 tablespoons icing sugar
1 teaspoon ground cinnamon
6 cardamom pods
3 tablespoons whole milk

For the mint grapes
45g caster sugar
15g fresh mint leaves
1 lime, zest only
500g mixed seedless grapes, halved and frozen

Start by toasting the pecans in a non-stick frying pan over a medium to high heat, making sure to stir all the time. This should only take a few minutes. This will really help to ramp up that nutty flavour. Take off the heat and put straight onto a chopping board, then roughly chop.

Put the yoghurt into a bowl and mix with the icing sugar and ground cinnamon.

Crush the cardamom pods and remove the green outer shells, then put the black seeds into a pestle and mortar and crush to a fine powder. Add to the yoghurt and give everything a good mix with the milk.

Add the yoghurt to a plate and swirl into an even layer. Sprinkle over the pecans.

Now make the mint grapes by adding the sugar along with the mint leaves and the lime zest into the pestle and mortar and crushing to a mixture that resembles wet sand.

Dot the halved frozen grapes all over the yoghurt and top with the minted lime sugar.

+ If you have an abundance of nuts in the house, don't store them in the cupboard. Store them in a zip-lock bag in the freezer, defrost and use them as you would usually in any recipe. They keep longer in the freezer than in the cupboard. No more wasted nuts!

Oats took me a while to enjoy. The blandness of oats when I ate them for the first time was alarming, but if oats are shown a little bit of love, they don't have to be boring. These oats are toasted with bay and have all the flavour you could imagine.

Roasted Toasted Oats

serves

4

Take a medium non-stick pan and pop over a medium heat. Add your rolled oats and fresh bay leaves and begin toasting till the oats are a deep golden colour and you can really smell the bay. Be sure to stir all the time, moving the oats so they don't catch and burn.

Add the coconut oil and stir through. Now add the coconut milk and water, mix and leave to simmer over a low to medium heat till thickened, making sure to stir all the time. Add the caster sugar and stir through and cook for a further 5 minutes.

Now make the topping by adding the berries to a bowl with the golden syrup, water and vanilla. Mix through and you are ready to serve your toasted oats with the berries on top.

Cook: 20 minutes

For the oats
160g rolled oats
10 fresh bay leaves
3 tablespoons coconut oil
400ml coconut milk
300ml water
75g caster sugar

For the topping
200g mixed berries
25g golden syrup
1 tablespoon water
½ vanilla pod

+ If you are not sure about whether your oats are toasting, keep some untoasted oats beside you while you stir, so in the moment where you think, 'This isn't even toasting,' you will clearly see it is.

We have always had our scrambled eggs cooked to within an inch of their lives. I love a runny egg, so why not a runnier scrambled egg? But when I say runny, I mean running off the plate, almost like a custard. These velvety scrambled eggs are spiced with cumin and seasoned with chilli salt and are the best way to start a day.

Velvet Eggs on Toast

serves

Prep: 6 minutes
Cook: 13 minutes

3 tablespoons butter
2 teaspoons ground cumin
25g fresh chives, finely chopped
100ml whole milk
6 medium eggs

For the chilli salt
6 tablespoons fine salt
6 tablespoons chilli powder

To serve
sliced bread, toasted
butter, to spread

Start by adding the butter to a medium non-stick pan over a medium heat. Wait for the butter to melt to a liquid and as soon as it has started to froth and get bubbly, add the ground cumin. Take off the heat and stir through, so the flavours are released without burning the spices.

Add the chopped chives to a bowl along with the milk and eggs and whisk through. The chives will float on top but don't worry about that.

Mix the salt and chilli powder together. Add a quarter of a teaspoon of the chilli salt to the egg mixture and save the rest in a jar for when you want a seasoning with a kick for all your other kitchen adventures.

Pour the egg mixture into the pan with the butter and put over a low to just slightly medium heat. Keep stirring using a spatula, moving the eggs all the time - we are not looking to fry the eggs, we are looking to thicken them. This should take 13 minutes and you will end up with eggs that are rich and thick but not overcooked.

Pour the eggs onto your buttered toast, sprinkle on some more of that chilli salt and it's time to enjoy your little-bit-different eggs on toast.

+ To make a savoury filling for your parathas instead of sweet (see page 24), you could cook these eggs over a high heat until fully cooked. Cool them completely, mash up to remove any big lumps and then use as a filling.

Vermicelli pudding is a go-to Sunday breakfast in our home and is mostly eaten during special occasions or when guests come over. But why save something as good as this for that – it should be enjoyed way more than just at select times or for select people. The pudding is cooked and set in a tin, cut into squares and finished with a crunchy, sugary top. Unconventional, yes, but conventional is boring and these slices are not!

Vermicelli Slices

makes

16

Prep: 8 minutes

Cook: 20 minutes (+ chilling)

1 large cinnamon stick

1 bay leaf

4 cardamom pods, squashed to expose the insides

200g vermicelli noodle nests

65g salted butter

600ml double cream

100g caster sugar

100ml water

50g demerara sugar

Put a medium non-stick pan over a medium to high heat, add the cinnamon stick, bay leaf and the squashed cardamom pods and stir till you can smell the aroma.

With the vermicelli noodle nests still in their packaging, put the packet into another food bag and, using a rolling pin, smash the vermicelli into small strands till you no longer have big pieces.

Add the vermicelli to the pan with the whole spices and stir constantly on a high heat for about 7 minutes until everything is a deep golden brown. Now add the butter and stir through till the butter has melted.

Add the cream, caster sugar and water and bring to the boil to cook the vermicelli. As soon as it has boiled, lower the heat and simmer for 5–6 minutes, till the mixture starts to come away from the sides. Take off the heat.

Have a square 20cm cake tin lined with some baking paper ready. Pour in the mixture and flatten to an even layer. Leave to cool for 20 minutes, then chill for an hour in the fridge.

When you are ready to serve, lift out of the tin, place on a board and cut into 16 equal squares. Sprinkle over the demerara sugar and blowtorch the top to create a sugar-sweet crust. It will catch on the bits of vermicelli that are sticking up, but that will add to the flavour.

+ If you don't have a blowtorch, you can pop the squares onto an ovenproof tray and toast under a hot grill for a few seconds, just until the sugar has melted. You will get the exact same result as if you did it with a blowtorch.

Noon

We eat aloo, as in potatoes, in so many ways. Curried, fried, mashed, etc. Potato is a love language and it's never better than when it is spiced, fried and whacked in between a brioche burger bun to make a moreish aloo burger.

Aloo Burgers

makes

4

Prep: 18 minutes

Cook: 17 minutes

For the patties

400g readymade mashed potato

2 teaspoons ground cumin

2 spring onions, thinly sliced

2 chillies, thinly sliced

2 tablespoons chilli sauce (of your preference)

2 tablespoons mayonnaise

6 tablespoons dried breadcrumbs

1 teaspoon salt

1 medium egg

oil, for frying

To serve

4 brioche burger buns

baby spinach

sliced red onion

ketchup/mayonnaise

onion rings

For the patties, start by putting the mashed potatoes in a bowl and breaking it up so it's easier to mix all the other ingredients in.

Now, add in the cumin, spring onion, chilli, chilli sauce, mayonnaise, dried breadcrumbs and salt and mix through till evenly combined, then add the egg and mix together. Divide the mixture into four equal patties and mould each into a hockey puck shape. Set aside while you heat the oil.

Take a large non-stick frying pan or wok and add a thin layer of oil into the base. Heat over a medium heat. As soon as the oil is hot, add the patties and cook on one side for 7 minutes till crisp and golden, then turn over and cook for another 7 minutes.

Lay the base of the burger buns down, add your chilli sauce, now add your patty, add the baby spinach and sliced red onion. Put the bap tops on. Easy-peasy aloo burger.

+ This is such a great recipe to make kid-friendly. Simply remove the chillies from the recipe entirely, switch the chilli sauce for ketchup and then it's perfect for kids or anyone who doesn't like spice.

We like to eat with our hands and these chicken wings are perfect for that. Sticky sweet and simply spiced, these are mouthwateringly good and easy to make.

Chicken Wings

serves

Prep: 10 minutes

Cook: 12 minutes

For the garlic sauce

95g black garlic paste/normal garlic paste

100g ketchup

100g brown sauce

50g cornflour

3 tablespoons art masala (see page 12)

1 teaspoon salt

2 tablespoons dark brown sugar

50ml vegetable oil

30g fresh coriander, chopped

For the wings

1kg chicken wings

1 teaspoon salt

To serve

sliced red onion

Start by adding the garlic paste, whatever type you're using, to a blender jug along with the ketchup and brown sauce. Now add the cornflour, art masala, salt, sugar, vegetable oil and half the coriander. Blend till you have a mixture that is smooth.

Take the chicken wings and, using a sharp knife, separate into three pieces. Remove the tip of the wings and set aside (see tip), then separate the flat parts from the drumettes. Do this to all the wings.

Get a large non-stick frying pan or wok or two medium non-stick pans and pop over a high heat. Salt the wings then add with no oil (we don't need oil because the skin has enough oil to help fry these up) and cook, stirring occasionally, till they are fried and golden on both sides.

Now add the sauce and mix till the wings are totally covered. Cook the wings till they are sticky and the sauce has reduced completely.

Take the wings off the heat, add to a serving dish and sprinkle over the remaining coriander and sliced onion. Serve and get sticky.

+ Pop the wing tips into a freezer bag and add to any leftover bones to make your own broths, stocks and soups.

When I was growing up, a tiny pot of noodles was traditionally served as soon as dinner guests walked through the door. I used to think noodles were a right treat and you felt special if you were given them, knowing that dinner awaited. These days noodles don't feel like a treat, more like a given, but we still love them at any time of day. These are simply cooked with a delicious crispy crust to add to the flavour and texture.

Crispy Fried Noodles

serves

Prep: 12 minutes

Cook: 17 minutes

For the noodles

100ml oil

1 teaspoon ground turmeric

2 onions, chopped

1 teaspoon salt

3 x 90g packets of vermicelli noodles

3 medium eggs

½ teaspoon salt

3 green chillies, chopped

large handful of chopped fresh coriander

For the mayo

2 heaped tablespoons mayonnaise

1 tablespoon cold water

½ lime, juice only

1 clove of garlic, crushed to a paste

1 teaspoon curry powder

pinch of salt

Start by pouring the oil into a large non-stick frying pan. Add the turmeric and the onion along with the salt and cook over a high heat for 10 minutes till the onion is soft and brown.

Meanwhile, take the packets of noodles and break into pieces. Add to a bowl, pour over hot water and submerge the noodles till soft. Drain and set aside.

As soon as the onion is soft, turn the heat up to high and toss in the drained noodles. Cook the noodles until they are fully mixed together with the onion and have a rich golden colour from the turmeric.

Add the eggs to a bowl with the salt, green chilli and coriander. Mix to break up the eggs. Make sure the noodles are flat and in an even layer, then pour in the egg all over the noodles and gently mix so the egg sinks to the bottom.

Over a high heat, fry until the eggs are cooked and the bottom is crisp - this should take about 5 minutes. Turn off the heat and allow to sit in the pan to cool for a few minutes - this will help it turn out cleanly.

Now for the mayo - add the mayo, cold water, lime juice, garlic, curry powder and salt to a bowl and mix well.

Tip out the noodles onto a large flat dish, crispy-side up. Drizzle the mayo all over the noodles and you are ready to serve, eat and, most of all, enjoy.

+ If you want warmth without the fresh heat of the green chillies, try paprika to start with and work your way up to cayenne, then, if you're feeling braver, try chilli flakes, then chilli powder and finally perhaps go for the green chillies. Or leave them out entirely.

I grew up eating chicken livers. They were cheaper than meat to buy, but of course I didn't know that at the time – I was too busy enjoying them. We always ate them in curry form and as much as I love them that way, I also really love them cooked quickly but still packed to the brim with flavour.

Chicken Liver Grills

serves

4

Prep: 8 minutes

Cook: 10 minutes

400g chicken livers, drained and patted dry of any excess moisture

2 tablespoons ginger paste

2 tablespoons garlic paste

1½ tablespoons art masala (see page 12)

2 tablespoons chickpea flour

1 teaspoon salt

3 tablespoons vegetable oil

1 red onion, sliced

1 lemon, cut into quarters

To serve

sliced bread, toasted

butter, to spread

small bunch of finely chopped fresh chives

Take the chicken livers, making sure they are drained of any excess moisture, and pop them into a bowl.

Grab another bowl and add the ginger paste, garlic paste, art masala, chickpea flour, salt and oil. Mix well. Tip the chicken livers into the spice mix and stir through. Cover and leave.

Pop the grill on to the highest heat.

Add the onion to the chicken livers and mix through. Put the mixture in an even layer onto a baking tray. Add the quarters of lemon to the tray on the side.

Grill for 5 minutes, take out and give everything a good mix, then grill for another 4–5 minutes.

Take out and serve the chicken livers on the buttered toast with the juice of the softened lemons squeezed right on top. Sprinkle with the chives and eat while hot.

+ If you wanted to do something a little bit different with the livers, you could add 150g melted butter to the fully cooked livers and whizz into a smooth pâté to serve on toast in a different way altogether.

LODGE

This is a traditional way of using up leftover rice and we often eat it for breakfast, using rice from the night before. But this is so good you don't need leftovers – make it using a packet of pre-cooked rice and have it for lunch.

Egg Fried Rice

serves

4

Prep: 10 minutes

Cook: 25 minutes

For the eggs

2 tablespoons oil

4 medium eggs

½ teaspoon salt

1 teaspoon chilli powder

For the rice

150g butter

2 onions, sliced

1 tablespoon curry powder

½ teaspoon salt

500g cooked rice, out of a packet or leftover rice from the night before

To serve

large handful of chopped fresh coriander

50ml olive oil

3 green chillies

½ lemon, juice only

1 teaspoon honey

Start with a large non-stick frying pan or wok and pop over a high heat with the oil.

Add the eggs to a bowl with the salt and chilli powder and give it all a good whisk. Pour the mixture into the hot oil and whisk the eggs till fully cooked, like scrambled eggs done well. Transfer the eggs to a plate and pop the pan back over a high heat.

Put the butter into the pan and wait for it to melt and begin to get frothy. As soon as it does, add the onion and cook over a high to medium heat till very golden brown. Lower the heat and add the curry powder and salt with a splash of water. Allow the spices to cook till the water has evaporated completely.

Now add the rice – whether it is out of a packet or leftover rice from the night before doesn't matter, both will work. Cook the rice over a high heat till golden and starting to catch a little on the base. Add the cooked egg back into the pan and mix to combine. Take off the heat.

Before serving, use a pestle and mortar to crush the handful of coriander, olive oil, green chilli, lemon juice and honey down to a smooth green paste. Drizzle all over the egg fried rice and serve.

+ If you are worried about what to do with the other lemon half, you need not worry – take out the fleshy insides of the lemon, so you are left with just the hollow peel. Then put the lemon shell into a bowl and fill with bicarbonate of soda, pop it into the back of the fridge and this will leave it smelling fresh for weeks.

This is the perfect thing to eat when the weather is warmer. It is a great way of having greens and really, really enjoying them! The kale is softened with the magic of salt and citrus and all mixed together with simple tinned mackerel. This is the kind of thing my Nani would cook when she had an abundance of green leaves in the garden and one tin of fish in the cupboard.

Green Mackerel Salad

serves

Prep: 25 minutes

Cook: 18 minutes

For the salad

100g kale, washed and sliced

60g spinach, washed and sliced

1½ teaspoons salt

2 lemons, juice only

2 onions, thinly sliced

For the fish

2 x 115g tins of mackerel fillets in oil

1 teaspoon chilli powder

To serve

2 chillies, thinly sliced

large handful of chopped fresh coriander

Start by making sure the kale is washed, then slice it. Add the sliced kale to a bowl, removing any hard stalk pieces.

Add the sliced spinach to the bowl along with the salt and lemon juice.

Get your hands in and give everything a really good mix to make sure you are really softening it all and breaking down that kale so it doesn't need any cooking at all.

As soon as you have really gone for it, add the onion and mix through by hand. Leave to sit for 15 minutes.

For the fish, put a small non-stick pan over a medium heat and add the contents of the tins – the oil and mackerel. Sprinkle over the chilli powder and fry till the fish is crisp. As soon as it is, take it off the heat and leave it in the pan.

Take the kale mixture and squeeze one handful at a time until any liquid, even if it's a small amount, is removed. Pop the kale mixture into a serving bowl. Add the chilli and coriander, then the mackerel with all the oil and mix through until you have a delicious green mackerel salad.

+ A great way of storing spinach without it wilting is to add your bags of spinach straight into the freezer. As soon as they are totally frozen, crush them in the bag and you have spinach that is 'chopped' without chopping, plus it takes up a lot less space.

I first ate a kati roll eighteen years ago in an underground restaurant – that's all they served and boy did they serve it well. It tasted so memorable I now make them all the time at home. This version has thinly sliced beef with the zing of mustard in an eggy roll.

Kati Rolls

serves

4

Prep: 10 minutes

Cook: 22 minutes

For the beef

500g diced beef, thinly sliced
oil, for frying
2 cloves of garlic, grated
1 red onion, thinly sliced
1 teaspoon curry powder
1 teaspoon salt
2 tablespoons wholegrain mustard

For the kati rolls

8 small tortilla wraps
4 eggs
large pinch of salt

Make sure your beef is as thinly sliced as possible. Now take the oil and drizzle into a shallow pan until the oil is about 1.5cm high. When the oil is hot, add the beef a few slices at a time and make sure not to overcrowd the pan.

Fry until crisp then take out with a slotted spoon and put onto a tray lined with kitchen paper. Do this till you have fried all the beef. Take the oil off the heat.

Add the beef to a bowl along with the garlic, onion, curry powder, salt and the mustard. Mix with your hands and set aside.

Now for the kati rolls. Open your packet of tortilla wraps and set aside. Break the eggs onto a plate with sides and add a pinch of salt. Pop the same pan with the oil back onto a high heat. Have a plate lined with kitchen paper ready.

Dip a tortilla into the egg till totally submerged. Quickly fry in the oil till crisp and the egg on the outside is cooked – this will take seconds on both sides. Do this to all the wraps.

Now it's time to eat. Fill the eggy wraps with the mustardy beef, roll and serve.

+ If, like me, you don't like the smell of cooking oil in your house, the best way to eliminate it is to pop a tablespoon of coffee, along with a cardamom pod, cinnamon stick and bay leaf, into some water in a pan and boil for 10 minutes and the smell of oil will go.

Every culture has its soup, its penicillin. Well, we have many and this is one of my favourites. What I love about this is that it uses no spices at all. It's simple to make and really does feel like you have been revived after eating it.

Revival Fish Broth

serves

6

Prep: 3 minutes

Cook: 18 minutes (+ cooling)

2 tablespoons shrimp paste
½ teaspoon turmeric
1 teaspoon salt
1 litre water
6 cloves of garlic, grated
4 tablespoons fish sauce
1 Scotch bonnet chilli
1 onion, thinly sliced
3 lime leaves, thinly sliced
80g fresh baby spinach
1 courgette, thinly sliced
150g mangetout, halved
25g dill, finely chopped
300g raw prawns

Start by adding the shrimp paste and turmeric to a large saucepan with the salt and a splash of the water. Mix it with enough of the water so that the shrimp paste is no longer a clump. Now add the garlic and fish sauce and mix.

Take the Scotch bonnet and pierce to release the flavour and only some of the heat. Add to the pan with the onion and lime leaves. Now add the baby spinach, courgette and mangetout, bring to the boil and as soon as it has boiled, leave to simmer till the veg has cooked through.

Add the dill and raw prawns and bring to the boil one last time, then take off the heat.

Leave to cool for 30 minutes, allowing time for the flavours to develop. It's best eaten not piping hot. Serve and feel revived.

+ If you are struggling to find the shrimp paste, you can always use a flavoured curry paste of your choice, like Thai green curry, tom yum or even miso. It will change the flavour, yes, but it will still be totally delicious.

Kebabs are a staple in our home. They are something that everyone has their own recipe for and I have tons of different ways of making them. This recipe is particularly delicious as the lamb is bulked out with potatoes, onions and carrots to keep the kebabs moist and add a touch of sweetness. The sauce that goes alongside is also lovely.

Lamb Kebabs

makes

18–20

Prep: 15 minutes

Cook: 10 minutes

For the kebabs

1 onion, roughly chopped

1 small carrot, chopped

1 small potato, peeled and chopped

7 tablespoons chickpea flour

1 medium egg

3 tablespoons art masala mix (see page 12)

1 tablespoon fine salt

450g lamb mince

oil, for frying

For the dip

3 cloves of garlic

large handful of fresh coriander

large handful of fresh mint

pinch of salt

½ teaspoon sugar

250g Greek yoghurt

For the kebabs, start by adding the onion, carrot and potato to a blender and whizz till you have a ground mixture. Now add the chickpea flour, egg, art masala mix, salt and lamb mince and whizz until you have an even paste.

Have a bowl ready with some oil to cover your hands in to stop the mixture from sticking to them when you go to shape the kebabs.

Now, make the dip by adding the cloves of garlic, coriander, mint, salt and sugar to a blender or pestle and mortar. Once you have a crushed mixture, add it to a serving dish with the yoghurt and you have the perfect dip to go with your kebabs.

Add the oil to a large non-stick frying pan or wok till you have covered the whole base ready for shallow frying.

As soon as the oil is hot, cover your hands in the cold oil from the bowl and make 18–20 equal mounds. The mixture is sticky, so once you have your portions, shape as you go and start frying on a high to medium heat. They will need minutes on each side. Do this till you have fried them all. Serve the kebabs with the dip.

+ These kebabs freeze well and make great burger fillers. So, once they have been cooked and cooled, freeze them in a freezer bag. To cook, you can reheat from frozen in an oven or air fryer. I would totally make a double batch of these just so you can freeze them!

We love roast chicken – it's full of flavour and I often cook it in pieces as opposed to a whole chicken. However, I love the idea and ease of doing a whole chicken. This has flavour from the skin all the way to the bones and everything is cooked in one tray.

Rocking Roast Chicken

serves

4–6

Prep: 15 minutes

Cook: 1 hour 35 minutes

For the chicken

100g ghee

3 tablespoons ginger paste

3 tablespoons garlic paste

3 tablespoons art masala (see page 12)

1 tablespoon salt

2kg whole chicken

For the cabbage

½ cabbage, thinly sliced

2 carrots, grated

1 teaspoon ground turmeric

pinch of salt

For the gravy

1 onion, quartered

500ml boiling water

3 heaped tablespoons onion granules

pinch of salt

30g fresh chives, finely chopped

Start by making spiced ghee. Add the ghee to a small pan and melt till hot. Add the ginger and garlic pastes and mix while sizzling. Take off the heat and add the art masala and salt and pop into the fridge to harden enough to be able to spread by hand.

Preheat the oven to 180°C and have a baking tray at the ready. Using your hands, tease the chicken skin so that it comes away from the flesh so you create a pocket in which to add the spiced ghee. As soon as you have created that space, take the ghee in your hand and tease into the pockets so it sits under the skin and over the flesh. Spread any remaining ghee over the top of the skin and the legs and wings. Take the quartered onion, stuff it into the chicken cavity and seal the cavity using toothpicks.

Add the cabbage and grated carrot to the base of the baking tray. Sprinkle over the turmeric and salt and mix through. Create an even layer with space in the centre for the chicken to sit. Pop the chicken in the centre, breast-side down.

Roast for 1 hour. Turn the chicken over breast-side up, then stir the cabbage and roast for another 30 minutes.

Take out of the oven and add the cabbage to a serving bowl. Remove the toothpicks and put the chicken on a board ready to carve. Take out the cooked onion. Add it to a jug with the boiling water, sprinkle in the onion granules with the salt and whizz with a hand blender. Stir in the chives and serve the gravy with the roast chicken and cabbage.

+ Add the bones left over from the chicken to a large pan with 1 litre of cold water and boil till the liquid has reduced to 500ml. Strain and remove all the bones. Leave the liquid to cool completely, then pop into the fridge or freezer and you have home-made flavourful chicken stock.

This is a classic fish and onions dish that needs very little work. Rather than use exotic fish that has clocked up more air miles than the Kardashians, I try to opt for sustainable fish – whatever has the blue label of approval – and for this recipe I like to use salmon. It's an oily fish that works so well with these simple spices and sweet onions.

Spicy Salmon and Onions

serves

Prep: 15 minutes

Cook: 12–15 minutes

For the onions

oil, for frying

4 cloves of garlic, thinly sliced

4 onions, thinly sliced

1 teaspoon salt

6 green chillies, sliced lengthways

large handful of chopped fresh coriander

For the fish

4 salmon fillets, skin on (480g approx.)

6 tablespoons oil

1 teaspoon fine salt

1 teaspoon ground turmeric

2 teaspoons chilli powder

1 tablespoon butter

1 lime, juice only

Start by frying the onions as they take a long time to cook gently. Pour some oil into a large non-stick pan. Add the garlic and fry till golden. Add the onion slices with the salt and cook over a medium to high heat until the onions are soft and brown.

Meanwhile, on to the salmon. Add the salmon to a tray and drizzle over the oil. Sprinkle over the salt, turmeric and chilli powder and use your hands to make sure the fish is covered entirely in the colourful mix.

As soon as the onions are golden, add to a serving dish with the sliced green chillies and sprinkle over the coriander.

Put the same pan you cooked the onions in back onto a high heat. As soon as the pan is hot, add all the fish skin-side down. Once the fish is down don't move it. Pour in any extra oil from the tray. Cook for 3 minutes and then turn over and cook for another 3 minutes on the other side.

As soon as they are cooked, add the fillets, skin-side up, onto the onions.

Put the pan back on the hob, add the butter and let it melt. Squeeze in the juice of the lime and let it bubble up, then drizzle over the salmon and onions.

+ If you do not have any citrus at home – lemons or lime – you can use a tablespoon of white or malted vinegar instead.

Prawns need very little work, but as they take such a short time to cook, all the work must go into creating a simple and delicious sauce for the prawns to be enveloped in. This sauce is rich, tomatoey and tangy.

Tangy Tomato Prawns

serves

4

Prep: 6 minutes

Cook: 25 minutes

100ml olive oil
4 cloves of garlic, thinly sliced
6 tomatoes, finely diced
1 teaspoon salt
1 lemon, juice only
1 teaspoon ground turmeric
2 teaspoons chilli powder
3 teaspoons tamarind paste
450g raw prawns

To serve

large handful of chopped fresh coriander

Start by adding the olive oil into a large non-stick frying pan or wok. As soon as the oil is hot, add the garlic and fry till very golden.

Add the tomatoes with the salt and lemon juice and cook over a high heat for 10 minutes till the tomatoes are totally soft.

Now add the turmeric, chilli powder and tamarind paste and cook till the tomato sauce has started to come away from the sides of the pan. Add the prawns and cook till they are pink and have cooked into the C-shape.

To serve, take off the heat and sprinkle with a handful of coriander.

+ If you don't have fresh tomatoes, you can always substitute with tinned tomatoes, but as they are slightly more acidic, add a teaspoon of sugar to balance the acid and give a little sweetness.

Staples

I never ate biryani as a child at home, but it has become something that my kids have grown up eating and traditions must start somewhere. There are so many variations of biryani; this one is simple, using beautiful, sweet leeks.

Crispy Leek Biryani

serves

6–8

Prep: 25 minutes

Cook: 1 hour

For the rice

500g basmati rice

1.5 litres cold water

1 cinnamon stick

2 bay leaves

3 cardamom pods

1½ teaspoons salt

For the crispy leeks

150g ghee

200g leeks, sliced

fine salt, for sprinkling

For the soft leeks

50g ghee

5 cloves of garlic, grated

200g leeks, thinly sliced

1½ tablespoons salt

6 green chillies, pierced

4 tablespoons art masala (see page 12)

To serve

6–8 fried eggs

Let's start with the rice. Put the basmati into a large pan with plenty of room for the rice to boil, then add the water along with the cinnamon stick, bay leaves and cardamom pods. Put the pan over a high heat and bring the water and rice to the boil, then boil for 7 minutes. Take off the heat and drain into a sieve, leaving the whole spices in there. Rinse the rice under cold water till it is cold and leave to drain and cool on the side.

Now take the same pan, dry off any liquid and add the ghee. As soon as the ghee is hot, add the sliced leeks in an even layer. Leave to get crispy without stirring too much, turning occasionally so they get golden all over.

Have a plate ready with some kitchen paper and drain off the leeks as soon as they are crispy. Sprinkle generously with the salt so they keep their crispiness.

Pop the same pan back on the heat with another 50g ghee and allow to melt. Add the garlic and fry till golden. Add the leeks, salt and chillies and cook till the leeks are just soft.

Add the art masala and mix through, then cook over a mellow heat for 10 minutes before taking off the heat.

Take a medium non-stick pan and fill half the pan with the cooled rice, including any of the whole spices. Make sure it is an even layer. Add the soft leek mixture right on top in an even layer and then cover with the other half of the rice.

Cover the top of the pan tightly with clingfilm, firmly place the lid on and pop onto a low heat for 30 minutes. Take off the heat, remove the lid and clingfilm and mix the rice with the leeks.

Serve with a runny yolk fried egg and sprinkled with the crispy leeks.

+ You can use frozen sliced onions if you cannot find leeks or are in a rush. They work just as well and having some frozen onions stashed in the freezer can be so helpful when you are in a rush.

When there wasn't enough rice cooked, we would resort to finding some bread in the cupboard and using that to be the sponge that soaked up our curry. But it doesn't have to be a rice emergency-type situation, you can just make these rolls to eat with your dinner – perfect for soaking up anything delicious.

Dinner Rolls

makes

Prep: 17 minutes (+ proving)

Bake: 20 minutes

For the dough

500g plain flour, plus extra for dusting

14g fast-action yeast

1 teaspoon salt

2 tablespoons caster sugar

30g unsalted butter, softened

375ml lukewarm whole milk

oil, for greasing the tray

For the butter

75g unsalted butter

½ teaspoon salt

1 tablespoon art masala (see page 12)

Begin with the dough. Add the plain flour to a bowl with the yeast, salt and sugar and mix through.

Now add the butter and use your hands to rub in. Make a well in the centre, pour in the warm milk and bring the dough together. As soon as you no longer have any pockets of flour left, knead the dough till it is smooth, shiny and stretchy.

Leave in a lightly greased bowl, covered, in a warm place to double in size.

Get a large baking tray, grease and line it and set aside.

Take the dough and tip it out onto a lightly floured worktop and knock out all the air bubbles. Now divide the dough into 12 equal balls and place on the tray, leaving a little space between them to grow.

Once you have laid them on the tray, cover with some greased clingfilm and leave to prove till the dough balls have doubled in size and the edges are just touching.

Preheat the oven to 200°C and bake for 15 minutes.

Meanwhile, melt the butter and add the salt and masala mix.

As soon as the dough balls come out and while they are hot, brush all over with the butter. Serve, tearing and sharing while piping hot and dipping into the remaining butter for extra flavour.

+ You can use wholemeal flour if you want for these rolls, but you may need extra liquid (milk) as the bran soaks up more water.

Rice is the staple in our home – growing up and even to this day. If the kids could pick any dinner, it's always something with rice. So here is one of my favourites: simple rice, glistening with ghee.

Ghee Rice

serves

Prep: 8 minutes
Cook: 20 minutes

500g basmati rice
100g ghee
large pinch of salt

Start by washing the rice. I like to do this in the pan I am cooking my rice in. Keep washing, swishing the rice gently, without crunching in your hands to avoid breaking them.

Drain the water, add more water, swish and repeat till your water is clear. It will always be a little bit cloudy but as soon as the rice is clearly visible, you can start cooking.

Fill the pan with cold water just 2cm above the rice – this works every time. Get a ruler out for the first few times and before you know it you won't need the ruler, you will just know.

Pop over a high heat and keep mixing it so the rice doesn't settle on the bottom. Just keep moving the rice till the water comes to a boil.

Keep boiling till the water has completely boiled off, then put the lid on, lower the heat to the lowest setting and leave to steam for 10 minutes.

Take the lid off after 10 minutes and add the ghee and salt. Use a fork to fluff up the rice and it's ready to eat.

+ This is a great recipe if you just want to cook plain rice with none of the frills. Just don't add the ghee when it's cooked.

These buttery parathas are filled with a delicious spiced pea mixture. These are the kind of thing we would eat when we went out dress shopping before Eid. This is my version, using peas. Traditional it is not, but it has become something of a tradition in our home.

Green Pea Parathas

makes

Prep: 20 minutes (+ resting)

Cook: 32 minutes

For the dough

600g plain flour

1 teaspoon salt

4 tablespoons vegetable oil

400ml tap warm water

For the pea filling

200g frozen peas, boiled and cooled

2 cloves of garlic, grated

pinch of salt

2 teaspoons curry powder

small handful of finely chopped fresh coriander

To serve

melted butter

Start by making the dough. Add the plain flour to a large bowl with the salt and oil and mix through. Now drizzle in the tap warm water and, using your hands, bring the dough together.

Tip out onto the worktop and knead very gently till you no longer have any floury pockets left. Don't be tempted to knead too much or this will create a stretch you don't need. Cover with the bowl and leave on the worktop for about 20–30 minutes to rest.

Make the pea filling by adding the peas to a bowl and crushing them to a rough paste. Add the garlic, a good pinch of salt, the curry powder and coriander, mix through and set aside.

Divide the dough into eight smooth balls and leave them under the bowl when you are not shaping them.

Take one dough ball and spread and flatten with the palm of your hands, pinching around the edges to create a cavity in which to fill your paratha with its peas. Add a heaped teaspoon of the pea filling into the centre. Bring the dough together into the centre, encasing the pea mixture into the ball.

Lay on a lightly floured worktop seam-side down and gently roll to about 20cm. Do this to all the dough balls.

Put a large non-stick pancake pan on the hob and heat over a medium to high heat. Add a paratha and cook gently on both sides, flipping over and making sure to press the paratha as it cooks with the spatula. Cook for 3–4 minutes on each side.

As soon as you take the paratha out of the pan, brush with the butter on both sides. Finish making the rest. I like to eat the first one and then deal with the rest!

+ If you are not eating all of these at once, you can freeze them between sheets of clingfilm and gently cook from frozen on a non-stick frying pan, as and when you need.

These are just like savoury pancakes, but more fun. The batter is made with chickpea flour, so it has lots of flavour, even with so few ingredients.

Lacy Rotis

makes

16

Start by sifting the plain and chickpea flours into a bowl - you will need a spoon to push any flour clumps through. Add the salt and mix through.

Make a well in the centre and add the eggs and milk. Drizzle in the oil and whisk till you have a smooth batter.

Put a 24cm non-stick pancake pan on a medium heat and as soon as the pan is hot, brush with some oil.

One tablespoon at a time, drizzle and swirl in the batter. You will need about 3-4 tablespoons per roti. Cook for 30-45 seconds till the top looks dry. Flip over and cook for another few seconds. Make all the rotis the same way, brushing the pan with a little oil as you make each one.

Prep: 8 minutes

Cook: 8 minutes

100g plain flour

100g chickpea flour

½ teaspoon salt

4 medium eggs, lightly beaten

250ml whole milk

2 tablespoons oil, plus extra for greasing

+ If like me you love making crepes on a Saturday morning, you could absolutely use the same technique to make these lacy pancakes if you fancied.

This is in no way traditional, but paneer doesn't always have to be paired with spinach. It works well in other ways and by other ways I mean in this loaf – grated. It adds a saltiness and a texture that are unique and really brings this simple loaf to life. I love to eat this sliced, toasted and buttered with ghee.

Paneer and Chilli Loaf

makes

Prep: 20 minutes (+ proving)

Cook: 45 minutes (+ cooling)

For the loaf

500g strong bread flour

2 teaspoons chilli powder

2 teaspoons ground cumin

7g fast-action yeast

2 teaspoons salt

2 tablespoons oil, plus extra for greasing

320ml lukewarm water

200g paneer, grated

100g crispy fried onions

For the glaze

1 egg yolk

½ teaspoon ground turmeric

1 tablespoon whole milk

Start by adding the flour to a large bowl with the chilli powder and ground cumin and mixing till combined. Now add the yeast, salt and oil and mix through, making a well in the centre.

Pour in the lukewarm water and bring the dough together. Now knead the dough till you have a dough that is smooth and stretchy. Pop into a bowl, cover in clingfilm and leave in a warm place for the dough to double in size.

Lightly grease the inside of a 900g loaf tin.

Uncover the dough and tip out onto the work surface. Press out the air and flatten the dough, then sprinkle all over with the grated paneer and onions and knead into the dough. Shape into a loaf and drop into the loaf tin seam-side down.

Cover in greased clingfilm and leave in a warm place until doubled in size again.

Preheat the oven to 220°C.

Take off the clingfilm, mix the egg yolk, turmeric and milk together to make the glaze and gently brush all over the top. Bake for 15 minutes.

Reduce the oven temperature to 170°C and continue to bake for another 30 minutes. Take the loaf out and tip onto a wire rack to cool completely.

+ This loaf crumbled into breadcrumbs makes for a delicious crispy topping on a fish pie, so why not give that a go if you have any left over.

These were only a staple growing up because I grew up in and out of Indian restaurants. So, a Peshawari naan was a proper treat – the soft dough filled with a sweet, nutty surprise filling was like nothing I had ever tasted. And I am still very enthusiastic about making and eating Peshwari naans today.

Peshwari Naans

makes

4

Prep: 20 minutes (+ cooling)

Cook: 4–5 minutes

For the filling

75g ground almonds

15g desiccated coconut

35g cashew nuts, roughly chopped

35g raisins, roughly chopped

75g caster sugar

1 large egg

pinch of salt

For the dough

240g plain flour, plus extra for dusting

1 teaspoon caster sugar

1 teaspoon salt

1 teaspoon baking powder

120g Greek yoghurt

2 tablespoons vegetable oil

50ml whole milk

To serve

melted butter

Start with the filling. Add the ground almonds to a non-stick pan with the desiccated coconut and cashew nuts. Toast till golden brown.

As soon as they are toasted, add to a bowl along with the raisins, stir through and leave to cool completely. As soon as they are cool, add the sugar and mix through.

Now add the egg and salt and mix till you have an even paste mixture. Divide the mixture into four equal parts, set aside and get on with the dough.

For the dough, add the plain flour to a bowl with the sugar, salt and baking powder and mix through. Make a well in the centre and add the yoghurt, oil and milk.

Mix everything till you have a smooth dough, kneading for just a few minutes. Divide the mixture into four equal mounds.

Take each mound and flatten it enough to fill with the almond mix. Bring the edges into the centre, pinching as you go so you encase the sweet mixture. Roll to a roughly 15cm oval shape.

Pop a non-stick frying pan over a low to medium heat and as soon as the pan has heated, gently place a dough oval on top. Cook gently, covered with a lid, for a few minutes till lightly golden.

Flip over and cover again for a few minutes till golden on the other side, then take out and brush generously with melted butter so it soaks in. Do this with the rest of the naans and they are ready to enjoy.

+ If you don't have ground almonds at home you can take any nuts and grind to a powder. This will work just as well and create a unique flavour, depending on what nuts you use.

These remind me of when we used to have chapatis for dinner and I would insist on having mine deep-fried because I have always loved a deep-fry. They are like thinner, crispier chapatis, which are fried to puffy perfection.

Pooris

makes

16

Prep: 15 minutes (+ resting)

Cook: 25 minutes (4-5 minutes per poori)

250g plain flour, sifted

½ teaspoon salt

2 tablespoons oil, plus extra for your hands and greasing

water

oil, for frying

Start by adding the flour to a bowl along with the salt and oil and mixing through.

Now, make a well in the centre and slowly start adding water, mixing at the same time. We are not after a sticky soft dough. Quite the opposite, we are after a tight, dry dough. So, add the water a little at a time, making sure not to knead.

As soon as you have a smooth dough ball, get some oil on your hands and lightly smother the dough ball with oil. Cover and leave to rest for a minimum of 30 minutes.

Take out and divide the dough into 16 equal balls, rolling in your hands to make smooth balls, then place back in the bowl and cover.

Cover the worktop very lightly with some oil and roll a dough ball out to about 10cm. I like to roll out a few pooris and then fry and repeat.

Now get the oil into a deep, heavy-bottomed saucepan or deep-fat fryer, making sure the oil is about a third of the way up. As soon as the oil is hot, add your pooris in gently. Allow to fry and they will naturally puff up. You can also encourage the puff by taking the hot oil and drizzling it on top.

Drain the pooris upright in a colander, so you can keep that puff and drain some oil. Keep going until you have fried them all.

+ If you don't want to fry these, you could very easily dry-fry them in a pan. You won't get the same texture or flavour, but you will get a great basic chapati.

This is a go-to recipe for when I want to make something all-in-one pot, packed with veg out of the freezer. It's so simple and delicious and perfect for midweek meals.

Pulao

serves

6

Prep: 8 minutes
Cook: 55 minutes

500g basmati rice
100g ghee
4 cardamom pods
4 bay leaves
1 cinnamon stick
2 onions, thinly sliced
1½ teaspoons salt
60g garlic paste
60g ginger paste
200g frozen mixed vegetables
boiling water

Start by washing the basmati rice. Wash and drain the rice till the water you are using to wash it runs clear (see page 70 for instructions). Then leave the rice to drain in a sieve or colander.

Get a large non-stick pan with a tight-fitting lid. Rice needs room, so the larger the pan, the better.

Add the ghee to the pan and heat over a high heat. Add the cardamom pods, bay leaves and cinnamon stick, stir and allow them to sizzle and brown slightly. Add the onion and salt and cook till the onion is soft and translucent.

Now add the garlic and ginger pastes along with the frozen mixed vegetables and cook over a medium heat, allowing the veg to thaw out and cooking out any excess moisture. Mix in the drained rice, cooking for 5 minutes in the vegetable mixture.

Pour in the boiling water until it comes 2cm above the rice mixture. Over a high heat, cook the rice till bubbling, keeping stirring so the rice doesn't stick to the bottom. Cook till most of the liquid has evaporated and what you are left with is a liquid that is thick and starchy.

Stir the rice, level off, and lower the heat completely. Leave the rice to steam with the lid on for 15 minutes.

Take the lid off, fluff up the rice and it's ready to serve.

+ Mark a wooden spoon with a 2cm marking on the handle and use that every time you are cooking rice. You will get your rice bang on perfect every time.

These are traditional rotis that we eat only a few times a year, but that doesn't stop me – I love making and eating them. What I love about them is that they have a totally neutral flavour, which means they are a great carrier for whatever you are serving them with.

Rice Rotis

makes

16

Prep: 55 minutes (+ cooling)
Cook: 30 minutes

1 litre water
2 teaspoons salt
450g ground rice/rice flour
200g plain flour
oil, for greasing

Add the litre of water to a medium non-stick pan with the salt. Bring the water to a boil.

Sift the ground rice/rice flour with the plain flour.

Reduce the heat of the water and as soon as the bubbles settle, add in the rice and flour mixture. Stir immediately till you have an even mixture and no pockets of flour. Lower the heat completely, cover and leave to steam for 15 minutes to cook the rice.

Take the lid off and allow the rice mixture to cool for 15 minutes, then tip out onto a lightly greased worktop.

Divide the mixture into two mounds and start kneading the dough till it is comfortable enough to handle. Once the dough is smooth, roll each ball into a sausage shape and divide each sausage into eight equal balls, so you should have sixteen balls. Cover the balls with clingfilm while you roll them out in batches.

On the lightly greased surface, roll each dough ball into a thin round.

Put a non-stick frying pan on the hob over a medium heat and cook the rotis for a few minutes on each side till you start to see light scorch marks on them. Do this in batches, making a few rotis at a time until all are cooked.

+ This dough has a neutral flavour, so it doesn't take away from what you are serving the rotis with. You can even serve them as a dessert with fruit, chocolate spread, nuts, cream and honey, etc. – it's super-versatile.

Middle of the table

This is a great way to cook chicken, getting it tender and moist while it sits in spicy yoghurt to marinate. Perfect for dinner; perfect for a barbecue!

Yoghurt Chicken

serves

Prep: 10 minutes (+ marinating)

Cook: 45 minutes

250g Greek yoghurt
3 tablespoons vegetable oil
1 onion, quartered
95g ginger paste
95g garlic paste
large handful of fresh coriander
6 tablespoons art masala mix (see page 12)
1 teaspoon salt
1kg chicken drumsticks
oil, for roasting
100ml water

To serve
5cm ginger, peeled and cut into strips
chopped red or green chillies
lemon wedges

For the marinade, start by adding the yoghurt and oil to a large bowl. To a blender add the onion, ginger and garlic pastes. Tear up the coriander and add that too along with the art masala mix and salt. Blend to a paste. Now add that to the yoghurt and mix well.

Take a sharp knife and cut three slits into each drumstick right to the bone so the marinade can get in. Add the drumsticks to the bowl, making sure to get your hands in to coat the drumsticks in yoghurt.

Cover and leave to marinate in the fridge for a few hours.

Preheat the oven to 180°C and drizzle some oil into a roasting dish.

Take the chicken out of the fridge, remove any excess yoghurt marinade and put the drumsticks into the dish. Drizzle with some more oil and bake for 35 minutes, making sure to turn halfway.

Use up the leftover marinade by adding some oil to a large non-stick frying pan or wok. Heat the oil and then add the marinade mixed with the water and cook until the mixture is thicker and darker.

Take the chicken out of the oven and toss it in the thick sauce. Sprinkle over the ginger strips and chilli and serve hot with lemon wedges.

+ Slashing the flesh of chicken pieces on the bone when marinating or cooking a curry not only allows the flavour to permeate through but also helps the chicken to cook faster.

Cooking whole fish from gill to flippers is something that I have grown up doing, but I absolutely get that it can be daunting for anyone who has never done it before. So let me guide you through making this wonderfully tangy tomato dish using every bit of the fish.

Whole Salmon Masala

serves

Prep: 15 minutes

Cook: 1 hour 20 minutes

For the fish

2.5kg whole salmon

100ml vegetable oil, plus more for frying

2 teaspoons chilli powder

1½ teaspoons ground turmeric

1 teaspoon salt

500ml water

For the sauce

10 cloves of garlic, crushed

400g tin of chopped tomatoes

2 teaspoons chilli powder

1 teaspoon ground turmeric

2 teaspoons salt

To serve

handful of chopped fresh coriander

green chillies, halved

Begin preparing the fish by making sure there are no scales. If you don't have a scale remover, you can remove using a spoon. Simply scrape against the direction of the scales and you will see them come right off. It's important to make sure all the scales are removed. Wash the fish and pat dry. Take off the head and tail and set aside. Cut the fish into 2-3cm thick steaks.

Add your oil to a large tray or bowl. Sprinkle in the chilli powder, turmeric and salt and mix in. Add the fish steaks and, using your hands, spread the spicy mixture all over the fish pieces.

Put a large non-stick frying pan or wok over high heat. Have another tray ready to put your fried salmon in when you are done frying the pieces.

Add a glug of oil into the hot pan and start by frying the head and tail. We are just frying till we get a little colour on the pieces and this should only take a few minutes on either side. Once the head and tail are fried, add to a medium to large-size saucepan. Pour the water into the pan and put over a high heat. As soon as the water comes to a boil, simmer for 15 minutes and then take off the heat.

While that is happening you can be frying the salmon steaks, again over a high heat, till they are crispy and have a golden scorched colour on the outside. You may find you will have to do this in batches and that's fine. Remove to the tray.

For the sauce, add some more oil to the frying pan. As soon as the oil is hot, add the crushed cloves of garlic and cook till just golden. Add the tomatoes, chilli powder, turmeric and salt and cook over a medium heat.

→

Meanwhile, drain and reserve the liquid from the fish head and tail then pour into a blender. Take the fish head and tail, gently remove any flesh and skin and add these to the blender, then get under the gills to remove any tender fish pieces and add these too. Discard the bones.

Blend, then add the mixture to the tomato sauce and cook until it is thick and coming away from the sides.

Add the fish steaks and any oil or water that might be in the tray. Coat in the sauce, cover and cook on a simmer for 20 minutes.

Sprinkle over the coriander and chillies to serve.

+ If you are not comfortable handling and cutting fish, you can always ask your fishmonger or the person at the fish counter to prepare the fish exactly as you want it. That's what they are there for and they're always happy to help.

This spiced keema mixture is normally eaten in a samosa or a spring roll, but it works just as well in a pie. And it isn't a tough pie to make. Using ready-rolled pastry it can be made on a dinner plate and is simple, easy and not daunting in any way. Don't let its simplicity fool you though – every layer is perfect!

Keema Plate Pie

serves

Prep: 35 minutes

Cook: 50 minutes (+ cooling)

For the filling

2 tablespoons vegetable oil

2 cloves of garlic, crushed

1 onion, finely diced

1 teaspoon salt

450g lamb mince

3 tablespoons art masala mix (see page 12)

400g tin of butter beans, drained

2 spring onions, thinly sliced

small handful of fresh coriander

For the pastry

2 x 320g packs of shortcrust pastry, ready-rolled

1 egg, beaten

1 teaspoon chilli powder

pinch of rock salt

Begin by making the filling to ensure we give it enough time to cool after cooking. Pour the oil into a non-stick pan and put over a medium heat. Add the garlic and cook till gently golden.

Add the onion, salt, mince and the art masala mix and cook till the mince is cooked through and any moisture from the mixture has dried out completely.

Take the drained butter beans, pour into a bowl and squash the beans using the back of a fork until they are completely mushed up. Add the mushed-up beans to the mince and mix through till you have a mixture that kind of comes together. Leave to cool completely.

Now, on to the pastry. Preheat the oven to 180°C and put a baking tray into the oven to heat. Lightly grease a 23cm plate pie dish or an oven-safe dinner plate.

Take out one sheet of pastry and roll out until a little thinner and large enough to cover the base of the dish with some overhang. Trim off any excess overhang, leaving a 1cm rim around the edge. Mix the spring onion and coriander through the filling. Add the filling to the dish and level off the top.

Take the second pastry sheet and again roll out until thinner and large enough to fit the top with an overhang of about 1cm. Brush the edges of the pastry in the dish very lightly with the beaten egg and add your pastry lid on top. Press along the seam so the base and top meet and stick. Tuck the pastry inwards and under itself all the way around and pinch using your fingers or a fork all along the edges. Combine the egg and chilli powder and brush all over. Sprinkle with rock salt and then brush again.

Put into the oven on top of the tray and bake for 45–50 minutes till golden on top. Take out and leave to cool for 10 minutes, then serve straight out of the plate in big wedges.

+ Never throw out any leftover bits of pastry. Roll out the pastry, brush with melted butter and sprinkle generously with a mixture of ground cinnamon and caster sugar. Cut into strips and bake in the oven till crisp and golden. Why waste when you can make sweet snacks with the leftovers?

This is a great way to make a curry with seafood. Seafood curries are right there at the top of the list in terms of the curries I always cook and eat. So, this makes for a great alternative if you want to try something different. The smooth fish paste is dropped into a rich sauce that just gently steams these sweet seafood koftas.

Seafood Kofta Curry

serves

4

Prep: 4 minutes **Cook:** 36 minutes

For the seafood

165g raw king prawns

180g sea bass fillets, skin removed (see tip)

½ teaspoon ground turmeric

2–4 tablespoons oil

pinch of salt

For the sauce

oil, for frying, plus extra for greasing your hands

1 bay leaf

4 cloves of garlic, crushed to a paste

1 onion, grated to a paste

1 teaspoon salt

3 tomatoes, grated to a paste

1 teaspoon tomato purée

1 teaspoon chilli powder

2 teaspoons curry powder

150ml water

To serve

large handful of fresh chives, finely chopped

For the seafood, start by patting the king prawns and sea bass with kitchen paper to remove any excess moisture. Add to a food processor with the turmeric, oil and salt and blitz to a smooth paste. Take the paste out and leave in a bowl lined with some kitchen paper to remove any more excess moisture while you make the sauce.

For the sauce, add a large glug of oil and the bay leaf to a large non-stick frying pan or wok. Let the bay leaf sizzle for a few seconds. Add the crushed garlic and cook for a few minutes till golden. Add the grated onion, salt, tomatoes and tomato purée and cook till the mixture starts to come away from the pan.

Now add the chilli powder, curry powder and water and allow to come to the boil. As soon as it boils, reduce the heat completely.

Oil your hands and take big pinches of the fish paste, about the size of a walnut in its shell. There's no need to make them into nice balls, just gently drop these uneven pieces into the sauce. If you find you are running out of space, just shake the pan a little and some room magically appears every time. Keep doing this till you have used up all the paste.

Leave to simmer in the sauce for 10 minutes so the seafood steams in the heat, which seals the shape. Gently turn each ball around, or shake the pan and they should all turn at once, then steam for another few minutes and the dish is ready. Sprinkle over the chives and serve.

+ To remove the skin from a small fish fillet, simply place the fillet skin side up on a plate and pour hot water over the skin. Leave for 2 minutes and the skin should peel right off, leaving you with the fish intact.

This is the kind of dish that you often see being served up at an Indian restaurant and while it may look complicated, it doesn't have to be at all. This is like the Bengali stir fry you never knew you needed. It's spiced, fast and a feast for the eyes.

Saag Aloo Chicken Jalfrezi

serves

Prep: 12 minutes
Cook: 30 minutes

- oil, for frying
- 3 dried red chillies
- 4 cloves of garlic, thinly sliced
- 400g tin of cream of tomato soup
- 1½ teaspoons salt
- 4 tablespoons brown sauce
- 4 tablespoons art masala mix (see page 12)
- 2 red onions, quartered
- 2 red peppers, cut into large chunks
- 560g tin of potatoes, halved
- 200g cooked chicken
- 80g fresh baby spinach

To serve

- handful of fresh coriander
- 2 spring onions, thinly sliced

Put a large non-stick frying pan or wok over a high heat and drizzle a good amount of oil into the base. Throw in the dried red chillies and toast in the oil until they swell up. Lower the heat, add the garlic and toast till it turns a deep golden brown.

Pour in the tin of cream of tomato soup, add the salt, brown sauce and art masala mix and cook till the liquid thickens and is reduced by half. Add the red onion, red pepper, tinned potatoes and cooked chicken and stir in the sauce on a really high heat until everything is coated in the sauce and catching on the base of the pan. Take off the heat and stir in the spinach until just wilted.

Serve the curry immediately with the coriander and spring onion sprinkled over.

+ You can make this entirely veggie by taking out the chicken and adding the same amount of whatever vegetable you fancy.

This is the kind of curry that we would normally cook if we had very little at home to eat. It was the filler curry that got us through to the next day. How lucky were we to have something as delicious as this to tide us over? This curry is so tasty, with the tomatoey sauce clinging to the hard-boiled eggs.

Duck Egg Bhuna

serves

Prep: 10 minutes

Cook: 1 hour 10 minutes

6 duck eggs, hard-boiled, shells removed

oil, for frying

3 bay leaves

2 onions, finely diced

1½ teaspoons fine salt

2 tablespoons tomato purée

½ teaspoon ground turmeric

2 teaspoons chilli powder

2 teaspoons curry powder

100ml water

To serve

drizzle of cream

small handful of fresh coriander leaves

Start with your hard-boiled duck eggs and pat them dry with kitchen paper. Using a knife, cut a few slashes into the boiled egg white – this will allow the flavour of the sauce to permeate.

Drizzle some oil into a medium-size non-stick frying pan and heat over a medium heat. Add in your bay leaves and as soon as they sizzle, gently add in your eggs one by one. Cook on a medium to high heat, rolling the eggs around as they start to get some colour and texture. As soon as you have a bubbly crisp texture all over the eggs, gently remove and place them on a plate.

Now, cut the eggs in half lengthways and fry the flat edge of the eggs. Once you have fried them all and they have an even golden colour, set them aside on a plate.

Leave the bay in the pan and drizzle in another good glug of oil. Add the onion and salt and cook until soft. Use a potato masher to mash the onion down to a smooth paste.

Now add the tomato purée and cook through. Get the turmeric in, along with the chilli powder, curry powder and water and cook till the liquid has evaporated and the curry paste is thick.

Add the eggs and roll them around till they are covered in the sauce. Leave to cook with the lid on, over a low heat, for 15 minutes.

To serve, drizzle in a small splash of cream and sprinkle with coriander.

+ You don't have to use duck eggs. If you don't want to or if you can't find duck eggs, use 8 medium chicken eggs instead.

I didn't grow up eating crab – some people do, others don't – but I absolutely love the sweetness, which you can't really get from any other seafood. This natural sweetness is quite a wonder and it really does work well cooked with the slight crunch of the green beans and the simple spicing, making it a bhuna I cook time and time again.

Crab Bhuna

serves

Prep: 5 minutes
Cook: 25 minutes

- oil, for frying
- 4 cloves of garlic, crushed
- 2 red onions, finely diced
- 2 red peppers, finely diced
- 3 mild red chillies, finely diced
- 1½ teaspoons salt
- ½ teaspoon ground turmeric
- 3 teaspoons curry powder
- 180g green beans, finely sliced
- 3 x 145g tins of shredded crab meat in brine, drained

To serve

- large handful of chopped fresh coriander

Start with a large non-stick pan or wok and put it onto the hob over a high heat. Add the oil and as soon as it is hot, add the garlic and cook until golden.

Now add the red onion, red pepper and red chilli along with the salt, turmeric and curry powder. Add a splash of water and the green beans and cook till there is no liquid left.

Now add the shredded crab meat. As you add the crab meat, make sure you remove any excess moisture. A bhuna is meant to be dry so we want to avoid any excess liquid. Cook with the lid off over a high heat for 10 minutes.

Take off the heat, add the chopped coriander and mix through to serve.

+ If you have any leftovers, you can cool them down, add mayonnaise and mix together. This makes an excellent sandwich filler.

Shellfish and citrus are a match made in heaven. I only ever grew up eating seafood curried, but not today! This is a simple citrus marinade made from sweet clementines and smothered all over some juicy big tiger prawns.

Citrus Tiger Prawns

makes

8

Prep: 8 minutes (+ marinating)

Cook: 8 minutes

For the marinade

6 cloves of garlic

1 onion, roughly chopped

2 small clementines

1 teaspoon ground turmeric

2 teaspoons chilli powder

large handful of roughly chopped fresh coriander

150ml oil

1 teaspoon salt

For the prawns

500g raw tiger prawns, with heads and tails on

8 skewers

2 tablespoons olive oil

For the marinade, add the cloves of garlic to a blender with the onion. Cut the clementines across the equator and remove any seeds. Now add the halves to the blender, peels and all. Add the turmeric, chilli powder, coriander, oil and salt and blend to a smooth paste.

Put the prawns into a bowl, pour in the marinade and carefully toss together. Cover and leave to marinate for 4 hours in the fridge.

Skewer the prawns, reserving the marinade, so they are ready to fry on a griddle or in the oven.

Add the olive oil to a non-stick frying pan and as soon as the oil is hot, add the reserved marinade and cook until thickened and coming away from the sides. This should take a few minutes.

Grill the prawns for 2 minutes on each side until they are pink and a C-shape. When they are ready, smother the cooked sauce all over them.

+ This is a great recipe to do in advance. If you want to, just pre-prep the marinade the night before and leave it in the fridge.

Duck is one of my favourite game meats to eat. It has such a distinct flavour and texture, which makes it all the more special. I used to love visiting an aunt of mine in Bangladesh who had a duck farm and that was what we ate when we visited. We played with ducks, we ate duck and we took duck home. You will love this version of mine. It's not entirely traditional but it really celebrates duck's unique flavour.

Duck and Cabbage

serves

4

Prep: 18 minutes
Cook: 1 hour 5 minutes

4 duck breasts
1 cinnamon stick
2 bay leaves
3 cardamom pods
2 onions, thinly sliced
1 tablespoon salt
2 tablespoons garlic paste
2 tablespoons ginger paste
1 teaspoon ground turmeric
2 teaspoons chilli powder
2 teaspoons ground cumin
3 teaspoons curry powder
½ white cabbage, thinly sliced

To serve
handful of chopped fresh coriander

Let's start with the duck breasts. Remove the skin and pop it into a blender. Slice the duck breast into thin strips and set aside.

Once the duck skin has been blended, add to a large non-stick pan. Pop the pan onto a medium heat and allow the fat to come out of the skin. Add the cinnamon stick, bay leaves and cardamom pods and let them sizzle and release their flavour. Add the onion and salt and cook until soft.

Get the garlic and ginger paste into the pan along with the turmeric, chilli powder, cumin and curry powder and mix. Cook through for a few minutes.

Throw in the cabbage and cook over a high heat for 5 minutes. Reduce to a medium heat, cover, and leave to cook for 40 minutes. 15 minutes before the time is up, place the duck strips into the pan, stir and replace the lid.

Take the lid off and cook over a high heat for a final 15 minutes, allowing any excess moisture to evaporate. Serve with the chopped coriander sprinkled over.

+ If you will not be using the other half of your cabbage for a while, then slice it up and blanch in hot water for 3 minutes. Drain, cool and pop into a freezer bag. Remove any air so it takes up as little space as possible and freeze for up to a year.

A dhansak is a meat curry cooked with lentils and that is exactly what I want to share with you – a simple beef and lentil curry cooked as quickly as possible but still crammed with flavour. However, this is a dhansak in baked form, with onion mash on top and cooked in the oven.

Dhansak Bake

serves

8

Prep: 10 minutes **Cook:** 1 hour 30 minutes

For the beef
2 tablespoons vegetable oil
2 onions, diced
½ teaspoon salt, plus extra for the mash and eggs
1 teaspoon ground cinnamon
3 tablespoons curry powder
1kg diced beef, cut into 1cm pieces
400g tin of lentils
500ml water
4 tablespoons beef gravy granules

For the onion mash
1kg potatoes, peeled and roughly chopped
200g butter
200ml whole milk
3 tablespoons mayonnaise
2 cloves of garlic, grated
75g crispy fried onions
small handful of fresh chives, finely chopped
2 spring onions, thinly sliced
200g red Leicester cheese, grated

To finish
4 medium eggs

Let's start with the beef. Add the oil to a large pan and make sure the oil is hot before adding the onion and salt. Cook the onion till lightly brown and translucent.

Add the ground cinnamon, curry powder and beef and cook with the lid off for 20 minutes. Add the lentils and water and cook over a medium heat for 20 minutes till some of the liquid has evaporated. Add the beef gravy granules, lower the heat and simmer for 20 minutes, making sure to stir occasionally.

Now, on to the onion mash. Boil your potatoes until soft, then drain and pop back into the pan. Warm the butter, whole milk and salt in another pan till the butter has melted.

Start mashing your potatoes or put through a ricer for the ultimate smooth mash. Add the milk mixture, then mix in the mayonnaise and garlic. Add the crispy fried onions and mix through until they begin to soften in the warm mash. Add the chives, leaving just a few for the top, then add the spring onion and half the cheese, leaving the other half for the top.

Preheat the oven to 220°C.

Get a 30cm rectangular roasting dish and pour in the beef mixture. Now dollop in the mash. I don't like to smooth it out – I prefer to leave uneven dollops in places and create some craters for our eggs.

Bake for 40 minutes, then take out and crack in the eggs where you have spaces. Sprinkle over some salt. Add the remaining grated cheese and chives and bake till the whites of the eggs have gone white, leaving the yolks runny. Take out and serve while still hot.

+ If you are making this for the freezer, flatten out the mash so it's easier to store and leave out the eggs entirely.

This recipe is pretty special as it uses a whole lemon, which really brings this entire dish together. Thinly sliced beef cooked to perfection and perfectly spiced. Curries need not be laborious and this one is spectacular.

Beef Lemon Balti

serves

4

Prep: 15 minutes

Cook: 30 minutes

100ml vegetable oil
1 onion, diced
2 teaspoons fine salt
60g garlic paste
60g ginger paste
500g diced beef, thinly sliced
½ small lemon, thinly sliced
4 tablespoons art masala (see page 12)
250ml hot water

To serve

large handful of chopped fresh coriander
½ small lemon, thinly sliced

The thing that makes this a balti is cooking it in a wok, which changes the way a curry cooks. There is more space for the water to evaporate and the sauce to dry up, unlike in a pot that stews. Both methods are great, just different in good ways.

So, let's get a large wok and add the vegetable oil. Put it over a high heat, add the onion and salt, and cook till the onion has really browned. Add the garlic and ginger pastes and cook for a few minutes.

Get the diced beef in along with the lemon and the art masala mix, then stir on a high heat till everything is combined.

Add the hot water and really allow everything to boil – you want to keep cooking and stirring till there is no more visible water. Everything will have thickened, and the sauce should be coating the meat.

Sprinkle over the chopped coriander and the sliced lemon. I like to serve this dish straight from the wok.

+ If you haven't made this masala mix, I highly recommend it, but you can also use something you have made yourself or you may have some garam masala mix that you want to use up. I am not a fan of waste, so I highly recommend using that. But when you run out and need some more, make my art masala mix and you will never look back.

Korma as I know it is very different to the dishes that are served up in Indian restaurants. In our version, there is no cream and there are no nuts. This dish is simple and aromatic with whole spices and I want to share this authentic Bangladeshi recipe with you.

Chicken Korma

serves

Prep: 35 minutes

Cook: 40 minutes

250g ghee

4 cinnamon sticks

4 bay leaves

6 cardamom pods

4 onions, finely diced

1 tablespoon fine salt

125g ginger, peeled and roughly chopped

2 medium/large bulbs of garlic, peeled and roughly chopped

200ml water

8 chicken thighs, bone still in or boneless if you prefer

Start by adding the ghee to a large cooking pot with a lid. Pop it onto a high heat and add the cinnamon sticks, bay leaves and cardamom pods and allow to just sizzle.

Now add the onion along with the salt and cook on a low heat for 30 minutes till the onion is soft and mushy but with very little colour on it.

Take your chopped ginger and garlic and add them with the water to a blender. Blend till you have a smooth mixture. Add to the pot and cook over a medium heat till there is little very liquid left and you have a thick sauce.

Slash the chicken thighs with three slits, all the way to the bone, then add the chicken thighs to the pot and mix into the sauce. Put over a medium heat and leave to cook with the lid on for 30 minutes. Take off the lid and you are ready to serve.

+ If you ever struggle to find ghee or you have run out, you can always substitute it with unsalted butter.

Veg at the table

These are the king of roast potatoes. All the lusciousness of normal roasties, but with bags and bags of extra flavour from the turmeric and tamarind. I like my potatoes and there are a squillion ways to cook them, so let's keep experimenting till we find every single way.

Bombay Potatoes

serves

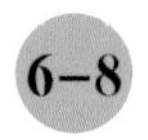

6–8

Prep: 18 minutes

Cook: 50 minutes

For the potatoes

1kg potatoes

2 teaspoons ground turmeric

3 tablespoons salt

To roast

150g ghee

2 tablespoons plain flour

2 tablespoons semolina

1 teaspoon baking powder

3 onions, quartered

1 bulb of garlic, cloves peeled and whole

salt

To finish

260g tamarind sauce

large handful of fresh coriander, chopped

Let's start with the potatoes by peeling and dicing them into 5cm chunks. Put the potatoes in a large pan with enough water to completely cover. Add the turmeric and salt.

Bring the pan of water to the boil and as soon as it's boiled, leave to simmer for 2 minutes, and then drain.

Preheat the oven to 180°C and put the ghee in a large roasting dish. Pop the dish into the oven and let the ghee and dish get hot.

Mix together the plain flour, semolina and baking powder. Add this dry mixture to the potatoes and toss them till covered completely.

Take the roasting dish out and add the potatoes in a thin layer. Season well and toss around in the ghee. Add the onion and garlic and toss around in the hot ghee.

Roast for 50 minutes, making sure to turn the potatoes around halfway through cooking. After 40 minutes, drizzle all over with the tamarind sauce before baking for the last 10 minutes.

Take out, sprinkle with the coriander and mix through.

+ When you peel your potatoes, don't throw away the peelings. Instead, add to a freezer bag and keep collecting all your peelings till you have a bagful. You now have enough to make a thick, hearty soup.

Daal, otherwise known as lentils, cooked gently for sustenance and comfort, is an absolute staple in our home and one of the first dishes I learnt to cook. There are so many variations, but I am sharing with you my fastest, yet still delicious, lentils.

Brown Daal

serves

4

Prep: 4 minutes

Cook: 55 minutes

For the daal

2 x 400g tins of brown lentils
1 litre cold water
100g hot lime pickle
1 teaspoon salt
3 bay leaves
1 teaspoon ground turmeric

For the tarka

100g unsalted butter
8 cloves of garlic, thinly sliced
1 onion, sliced
6 large dried chillies
2 teaspoons ground cumin

To serve

large handful of finely chopped fresh coriander

For the daal, start by having a large stock pot or dish at the ready.

Drain the brown lentils and rinse through a colander till the water runs clear and there are no bubbles or foam from the brining liquid in the tin.

Put the lentils in the pan along with the cold water, the hot lime pickle, salt, bay leaves and turmeric. Mix through and pop onto the hob to heat.

Bring to the boil and then leave to simmer, uncovered, for 40 minutes till the mixture has thickened. Make sure to stir occasionally, adjusting the heat as needed.

Now for the tarka. Put a frying pan over a high heat and put in the unsalted butter. Gently melt the butter till liquid. Over a medium heat, add the thinly sliced garlic and fry till golden.

Add the onion and chillies and cook till golden brown and the chillies have plumped up in the heat of the butter and are crispy-looking.

Take the tarka off the heat and add the ground cumin. Mix in well and toss the whole mixture into the lentils - you should get a sizzle as it drops in.

Mix well and serve with chopped fresh coriander.

+ For when you run out of onions or need a quick fix, stock up on crispy fried onions. Rehydrated they work well in cooking and they are also great as a crispy topping for any dish or salad.

Mango is delicious as it is, but when the flesh is charred it really brings out the flavour. Full of potassium and with loads of texture, this salad is simple and flavourful.

Charred Mango Salad

serves

4

Prep: 18 minutes

Cook: 15 minutes

1 large mango

1 red onion, thinly sliced

100ml apple cider vinegar

2 tablespoons caster sugar

250g packet of pre-cooked basmati and wild rice

1 teaspoon chilli powder

1 teaspoon ground cumin

large handful of chopped fresh coriander

100g cashews, roasted and roughly chopped

Start with the mango. We have to char this mango and we can do it in one of many ways. You can pop it under a grill and keep a watchful eye on it, moving it as it chars. You can pop it straight onto a gas hob and turn as the skin blackens. Or you can use a blowtorch to blacken the skin completely. As soon as the skin is black, leave to cool.

Take the red onion and add the apple cider vinegar along with the caster sugar to a small pan. Pop onto a high heat, bring to the boil and simmer for 5 minutes, then take off the heat. Drain and leave the liquid aside - save in a jar or bottle.

Chop the mango – flesh, skin and all – into cubes and pop into a bowl. Add the onion.

Heat the packet of basmati and wild rice as per the instructions and add to the bowl.

Sprinkle in the chilli powder and ground cumin and mix through. Stir in the coriander. Add the cashews, mix and it's ready to eat.

+ Keep the vinegar in a jar and add any leftover garlic and onion, etc. in to pickle. Or keep the vinegar to use in dressings for another time.

I always grow courgettes and while I think I can handle the rate at which courgettes grow, I can never keep up. So, after sharing my glut, this is one of my go-to recipes to make. Simply cooked with a few spices, toasted nuts and paneer, it's an all-in-one simple veg feed.

Courgette Paneer Pasta

serves

4

Prep: 15 minutes

Cook: 15 minutes

400g pasta shells

6 tablespoons ghee

225g pack of paneer, diced into 1cm cubes

100g pine nuts

6 cloves of garlic, crushed

500g courgettes, cubed into 1cm pieces

2 teaspoons fine salt

1 tablespoon ground cumin

2 teaspoons chilli powder

2 limes, zest and juice

30g fresh chives, finely chopped

Start by cooking the pasta shells as per the instructions on the packet in heavily seasoned water. While the pasta cooks, get on with the sauce.

Put the ghee in a large non-stick saucepan. When the ghee is hot, add the diced paneer and fry and toss the paneer till golden on all sides.

Lower the heat, add the pine nuts and toast those till they are a lovely golden brown. Add the garlic and cook through till brown.

Toss in the diced courgette and salt and cook till the courgette begins to soften. Now add the ground cumin, chilli powder, lime zest and juice and stir through.

Drain that pasta, reserving just 100ml of the pasta water. Add the pasta and the pasta water and cook over a high heat, stirring till all the liquid has evaporated.

Take off the heat, sprinkle in the chives and toss through.

+ If you can't find paneer, halloumi is a great alternative and can be used in the exact same way.

Think of all the watermelon rinds you have thrown away. That equals a lot of curries you could have eaten. The only part of the watermelon that cannot be eaten is the hard, thin green exterior, the rest of it is perfect for a curry, especially the rind. It's a cross between cucumber, water gourd and courgette, but is unique when cooked and spiced to perfection.

Watermelon Rind Curry

serves

Prep: 16 minutes
Cook: 42 minutes

1.5kg watermelon
4 tablespoons vegetable oil
1 large cinnamon stick
20g desiccated coconut
3 tablespoons crushed garlic
3 tablespoons crushed ginger
1 onion, diced
1½ teaspoons salt
1 teaspoon ground turmeric
1 teaspoon chilli powder
1 teaspoon ground cumin
1 teaspoon curry powder
300ml water
200ml coconut cream

To serve
50ml coconut oil
large green chillies
small handful of curry leaves

Let's begin by prepping the watermelon. Once you have taken the red flesh and diced and popped it into a freezer bag (see tip below), get on to the rind. Use a vegetable peeler to remove the thin dark-green skin and discard. Chunk the light green flesh into 1-2cm pieces.

Pour the vegetable oil into a medium non-stick pan, add the cinnamon stick and heat over a high heat.

Turn the heat down, add the desiccated coconut and toast gently. Now add the garlic, ginger and onion with the salt and cook down till light golden brown.

Add the turmeric, chilli powder, cumin and curry powder and mix through. Add the watermelon rind, the water and coconut cream and mix through. Bring to the boil and boil for 10 minutes.

Turn the heat down and leave to simmer for 30 minutes till the rind is soft and the liquid mostly evaporated.

Before you take the curry off the heat, pour the coconut oil into a small pan, add the chilli and curry leaves and, as soon as they start to pop, add to the top of the curry and serve.

+ If you are buying a watermelon specifically for this recipe, you will have a load of watermelon that you may not want to eat all at once, so freeze it in chunks. To make an instant watermelon gelato, add the frozen chunks to a blender with the zest of a lemon and lime and 200ml coconut cream and whizz.

These are the easiest greens you can make and the most delicious. They are nutritious and zingy and I make them at home and eat them at least three times a week. The best way to eat your greens is to actually enjoy them and these are more than enjoyable, they are delightful!

Greens

serves

4

Prep: 5 minutes

Cook: 20 minutes

125g cavolo nero/kale, washed and chopped

400g fresh spinach, washed

200g leafy greens, washed

10 cloves of garlic, thinly sliced

2 onions, thinly sliced

1½ teaspoons fine salt

1 Scotch bonnet chilli

150ml olive oil

Get a large pan ready so you can fit in all of these greens in one go.

Take the cavolo nero or kale and sift through, making sure to take out any very hard, stalky bits. If you find any, gather them together, then chop them down into manageable small pieces. Add it all to the pan.

Now take the spinach, slice in bundles and add it all into the pan. Take your leafy greens, cut into strips, then cut finely into thin pieces and add to the pan.

Add the sliced garlic cloves straight on top, then add the onion. Sprinkle over the salt. Pierce the Scotch bonnet and whack that straight on top too.

Drizzle over the olive oil and pop the lid on the pan. Place over a high heat and leave to steam for 5 minutes over a medium heat.

Reduce the heat and leave to steam for another 10 minutes. Give the greens a good stir to mix everything through.

Take the lid off and leave to cook over a medium to high heat till some of the liquid has evaporated. The greens are now ready to serve.

+ It's always worth having garlic granules at home for the occasions when you have run out. Garlic granules offer a similar zing to raw garlic, just a little less intense. They are worth having as a store cupboard staple.

These fries are like hybrid waffle fries, flavoured with chilli and curry powders and deep-fried. They are crisp on the outside and soft on the inside. I like to serve them with a squirt of sriracha and mayo.

Masala Fries

Makes

55

Prep: 4–5 minutes
Cook: 33 minutes

400g readymade mash
½ teaspoon salt
2 teaspoons chilli powder
2 teaspoons curry powder
1 medium egg
3 tablespoons chickpea flour
oil, for frying

To serve
½ teaspoon fine salt
1 teaspoon art masala (see page 12)
sriracha
mayo

Take your readymade mash and put in a bowl. Using the back of a spoon, break the mash up into a more pliable mixture.

Sprinkle in the salt, chilli and curry powders and mix till you have a mixture that is an even colour. Add the egg and chickpea flour and mix through. Pop the mixture into a disposable piping bag and set aside.

Pour oil into a frying pan high enough to shallow-fry. As the oil heats up, mix together the salt and art masala mix.

Cut the tip off the piping bag about 1cm wide and carefully squeeze the mixture out directly into the oil, using the scissors to cut the mixture when you get to about 7cm long. Keep going till you have a few in the oil.

Fry over a high heat for 3 minutes on each side till a dark golden brown. Drain on a tea towel lined with kitchen paper. Do this till you have fried them all.

To serve, drizzle the siracha and mayo all over and then sprinkle on the seasoning.

+ If you are worried about frying and having leftover oil, strain the oil through a sieve and save it in a small tub. If you save all your oil this way, after a few days the oil loses any food scent. You can then use it to waterproof things like wooden fences by brushing straight on.

Okra is a beautiful vegetable that can be cooked in a variety of ways to create really interesting textures. I love this saalom (curry) version, which is so easy to make and a total favourite. Smooth and spiced to perfection.

Okra Saalom

serves

4

Prep: 15 minutes

Cook: 1 hour 10 minutes

For the okra

420g fresh okra

1 litre cold water

1 teaspoon salt

For the sauce

200ml vegetable oil

6 cloves of garlic, crushed

2 onions, finely chopped

1 red pepper, finely diced

3 tablespoons garam masala

1 teaspoon salt

¼ lemon, finely diced, pith and all

large handful of finely chopped fresh coriander

Slice the okra into thin slices and add to the cold water along with the salt.

Bring the mixture to the boil and as soon as it does, leave to simmer over a medium heat, with the lid off, for 30 minutes.

Meanwhile, make the sauce by pouring the vegetable oil into a frying pan. As soon as the oil is hot, add the garlic and fry till golden.

Add the onion and cook till golden, then add the pepper, garam masala, salt and diced lemon and cook for a few minutes.

Stir the mixture into the okra, cover, and leave to cook with the lid on over a low heat for another 30 minutes. Take off the heat and sprinkle with coriander just before serving.

+ If you cannot find fresh okra, look in the international section of the frozen aisle in large supermarkets.

This is a salad that I have grown up eating. As a child, I remember not enjoying it at all, but now this is one of my favourite salads to eat. Lentils, not cooked, stirred with tangy lemon, zesty ginger and fresh coriander – refreshing and delicious.

Raw Yellow Lentil Salad

serves

After your lentils have soaked overnight, rinse them till the liquid runs clear. Set aside in a colander to drain completely, occasionally giving them a stir to remove any pockets of water that may be sitting between the lentils.

Put the fresh ginger in a bowl along with the onion, green chilli and coriander. Take the lemon and squeeze the juice into the mixture, then slice up the rind into thin pieces and add to the bowl too.

Mix with your hands to really macerate and develop the flavour. Add the lentils and salt and mix through. Serve with more lemon if you need an extra squeeze.

Prep: 18 minutes (+ soaking)

200g yellow lentils, soaked overnight

35g ginger, peeled and finely chopped

1 onion, finely chopped

2 green chillies, finely chopped

large handful of fresh coriander, chopped

½ large lemon or 1 small lemon

1 teaspoon sea salt

+ If you don't want to soak the lentils overnight, don't worry, there are so many lentils, beans and legumes that are pre-cooked and ready to eat. It's always worth keeping tins and packets of these in the house, so if you're feeling like you cannot be bothered to soak lentils, you have an alternative.

Rice is a huge staple in a Bangladeshi home and I love rice in any form, particularly rice paper. These are crisp fried baskets filled with a simple runny egg mixture.

Rice Basket Eggs

makes

Start with a pan with sides high enough to shallow-fry and large enough to fit the rice paper. Pour the oil into the pan and start to heat on a high heat.

Have your round rice paper sheets at the ready.

Take four small bowls, crack an egg into each bowl and sprinkle in the spring onion, a pinch of salt and chilli powder.

Add a rice paper round into the hot oil, immediately drop an egg in, allow to cook for about 30 seconds and then take out. Do the same to the other three and they are ready to eat.

Prep: 5 minutes
Cook: 2–3 minutes

oil, for frying
4 round rice paper sheets
4 medium eggs
2 spring onions, thinly sliced
chilli powder, to sprinkle
salt

+ If you cannot find rice paper you can do the exact same thing with readymade small tortilla wraps. They will take longer to fry and have a different texture, but they will be delicious all the same.

There is nothing traditional about pizza for me. This topping is simply a mixture of all the things I love – like smoky, spicy aubergine and creamy burrata – mashed up into one.

Smoky Aubergine Pizza

makes

Prep: 26 minutes (+ proving)

Cook: 45 minutes

For the dough

500g strong bread flour, plus extra for dusting

7g fast-action yeast

1 teaspoon sugar

1 teaspoon salt

20ml olive oil

300ml lukewarm water

For the topping

2 large aubergines

6 cloves of garlic, crushed

1 tablespoon ground cumin

6 anchovy fillets

4 tablespoons mayonnaise

2 teaspoons chilli powder

2 burrata

For the coriander oil

200ml oil

large handful of fresh coriander

pinch of salt

For the dough, start by putting the strong bread flour in a large bowl. Add the fast-action yeast, sugar and salt to the flour and mix to combine.

Make a well in the centre, pour in the oil and lukewarm water and bring the dough together. Knead the dough by hand or use a dough hook in a food processor to knead on a high speed till the dough is stretchy and smooth. Cover and leave in a warm place till doubled in size.

Meanwhile, make the aubergine topping. Preheat the oven to 220°C. Pierce the aubergines all over, pop onto a tray and bake till black all over.

Take the aubergines out and leave to cool slightly. Peel the skin and put the flesh into a food processor with the garlic, cumin, anchovies, mayonnaise and chilli powder and blitz to a paste. Set aside.

Take the dough out, tip onto the worktop and knead the air out. Divide the dough into four equal pieces, shape into round mounds and put onto a tray. Cover and leave to prove till doubled in size.

Dust the worktop and roll out the four dough balls to 20cm rounds, leaving a raised crust around the edges.

Divide the aubergine mix among the four pizza bases and smooth out into an even, generous layer. Take half a burrata for each pizza, tear and add to each pizza.

Bake the pizzas for 12–15 minutes till the edges have puffed up and browned. Do this in two batches if you don't have room in your oven.

Meanwhile, make the oil by putting the oil, coriander and salt in a blender. Take the pizzas out of the oven, brush the edges with the oil and drizzle more over the pizza.

+ I would highly recommend making a double batch of this dough and taking it to the stage of shaping the bases and then freeze them. You now have pizza bases ready for whenever you want to have fresh pizza.

Cauliflower isn't a vegetable we ate much in Bangladesh and when we did, it was often cooked in a curry with fish. I wanted to do something a little bit different, so here the cauliflower is baked and every crevice filled with flavour.

Whole Baked Cauliflower

serves

Prep: 30 minutes (+ cooling)
Cook: 65 minutes

For the cauliflower
1 large whole cauliflower, leaves on
1 tablespoon salt
1 teaspoon ground turmeric
50g ghee
1 tablespoon art masala (see page 12)
salt

For the filling
3 cloves of garlic
1 onion, roughly chopped
1 teaspoon salt
1 egg
100g chickpea flour
1 tablespoon art masala (see page 12)
2 tablespoons ghee

For the sauce
100g pistachios, plus extra chopped
1 tablespoon ghee
1 lemon, zest and juice
splash of water
1 teaspoon honey
1 teaspoon salt

Take the whole cauliflower, pop into a large stock pot and fill with water.

Add the salt and turmeric and pop the pot onto the heat. Bring the water to a boil and boil for 10 minutes. Drain the water and leave the whole cauliflower upside down for at least an hour until cool and drained of as much moisture as possible.

Heat the ghee in a pan and as soon as it melts, add the art masala and a little salt and mix through.

Take a large piece of foil. Put the cooled cauliflower in the centre and brush all over with the spiced ghee. Turn the cauliflower upside down and brush with the last of the ghee.

Now make the filling by putting the garlic, onion, salt, egg, chickpea flour, art masala mix and ghee in a blender and whizzing to a smooth paste. Pop into a disposable piping bag and cut a small hole.

Preheat the oven to 180°C.

Lift the softened, cooked outer leaves of the cauliflower and gently pipe the mixture into the holes and gaps till you have used up all the filling. Wrap up with the foil completely. Bake for 50 minutes.

Meanwhile, make the sauce. Put the pistachios, ghee, lemon zest, lemon juice, water, honey and salt in a blender and blend to a smooth drizzle.

Take out the cauliflower, remove from the foil and bake for another 15 minutes to get some colour on the cauliflower.

When cooked, slice the cauliflower, drizzle with the pistachio sauce and sprinkle with chopped pistachios to serve.

+ You can make this recipe completely vegan by using olive oil instead of ghee, maple syrup instead of honey and you can omit the egg altogether.

Stuff on the sides

Delicious vegetables and onion fried in hot oil, pakoras are a go-to when we want a snack. We usually make them at the end of the week when we have lots of veg knocking around to use up.

Back-of-the-fridge Pakoras

serves

Prep: 15 minutes (+ resting)

Cook: 5–6 minutes

2 onions, thinly sliced

300g thinly sliced veg (potatoes, carrots, courgettes, broccoli, cauliflower)

3 spring onions, thinly sliced

2 green chillies, sliced

¼ teaspoon turmeric

2 teaspoons salt

large handful of fresh coriander

300g chickpea flour

100–125ml water

oil, for frying

Put your sliced onion in a bowl and separate the onion strands. Add the thinly sliced veg.

Add the spring onion, green chilli, turmeric, salt and coriander, using your hands to mix the whole thing together and to soften the onion. Turmeric is notorious for staining clothes so wash your hands straight away after mixing. Cover and leave for 30 minutes. You will see some moisture being released from the onion mix, which is exactly as it should be.

Sprinkle in the chickpea flour and a little of the water and, using your hands, mix till you have a claggy dough that holds the veg together. Add more water if the mix is a little dry.

Pour some oil in a deep pan and heat to 180°C.

Take clumps of the mix with three fingers and gently drop into the oil. Don't be tempted to shape into balls. What we want are straggly pakoras that are crisp and uneven. Fry and turn in the oil till crisp.

Drain on a tray lined with kitchen paper. Fry the whole lot, eating as you go.

+ When deep-frying veg, all you must remember is that oil doesn't like water. To avoid the oil spitting, make sure not to use any veg that has lots of liquid in it, like mushrooms, tomatoes and cucumbers, etc.

There are only a few things cheesier than my Abdal's jokes, and this is one of them. Crisp, crunchy dough filled with spiced cheese that oozes out – stringy, deep-fried and delicious!

Cheesy Kachori

makes

10

Prep: 30 minutes (+ resting)

Cook: 18 minutes

For the pastry

300g plain flour, plus extra for dusting

1 teaspoon fine salt

3 tablespoons vegetable oil

175ml hot water from the tap

For the filling

150g Cheddar cheese, grated

2 tablespoons plain flour

2 teaspoons ground cumin

1 teaspoon chilli powder

oil, for frying

Let's begin with the pastry by putting the plain flour in a large bowl with the salt. Drizzle in the oil and rub it in.

Slowly add the hot water and bring the dough together by hand. As soon as the dough comes together and there are no more floury patches, shape it into a smooth ball. Be sure not to knead too much at all.

Roll into a sausage shape, divide the mixture into ten pieces and shape into even dough balls. Leave to rest on the worktop covered in a damp tea towel for 15 minutes.

Mix the filling together by putting the grated Cheddar in a bowl with the plain flour, ground cumin and chilli powder.

Now, take each dough ball and, on a lightly floured surface, roll out to approx. 10cm. Do this to all ten dough balls.

Divide the cheese mixture over the ten dough rounds. Take one, bring the edges into the centre and pinch to seal, pressing down so the dough and cheese are one. What you should be left with is a flat dough like a hockey puck. Now do the same to the other nine.

Heat the oil to 180°C and then lower to a medium heat. Add the kachoris a few at a time, making sure not to overcrowd the pan. Fry gently, turning till both sides are golden and crunchy. Lift out with a slotted spoon and drain on kitchen paper.

Fry them all and eat as soon as they are cool enough to handle.

+ Did you know you can freeze cheese? Freezing cheese is a great way of reducing waste. Grate it, pop it into a freezer bag and use it from frozen.

→

These are just like spring rolls but are filled with minced chicken, wrapped in crisp filo and baked. They are a great alternative to fried spring rolls.

Chicken Rolls

makes

14

Prep: 30 minutes

Cook: 25 minutes

For the filling

2 tablespoons ghee

3 cloves of garlic, grated

500g chicken mince

3 tablespoons art masala (see page 12)

1 teaspoon salt

2 red onions, diced

small handful of finely sliced fresh coriander

For the pastry

270g pack of filo pastry sheets

1 egg, beaten

75g ghee, melted

Start by making the filling. Put a non-stick frying pan over a high heat with the ghee. As soon as the ghee is hot, add the garlic along with the chicken mince and cook the mince till it has completely changed colour, is catching a little and toasting in places.

Add the art masala and salt and mix through for a few minutes. Take off the heat and add the red onion and coriander, mix in and set aside.

For the pastry, all you need is readymade filo sheets. Take the rectangular sheets and halve them so you have 14 squares.

Pile them up so they don't dry out and cover with a damp tea towel. Take one sheet at a time and put a heaped tablespoon of the chicken mix into the centre.

Fold in the two sides, the right hand and left hand, so the shape you are looking at is a rectangle. Fold the bottom bit of pastry over the chicken mince, all the while making sure you are shaping the mince and moving it so it is a tubular shape. Brush the flap of pastry remaining with the beaten egg and roll and you will have your roll.

Set aside onto a baking tray. Do the same with the rest of the pastry squares.

Preheat the oven to 180°C.

Brush the rolls all over with melted ghee and bake for 25 minutes, making sure to turn halfway. Take out and eat while still hot.

+ If you want to get a really smooth garlic paste, add a pinch of salt when you are grinding it down in a pestle and mortar, the salt granules give the garlic something abrasive to crush against to really get a great paste.

Okra is so often cooked – in fact, growing up I'd only ever known it and eaten it cooked. But it is absolutely delicious raw and you really get to appreciate the complex design of such a beautiful vegetable. The only thing cooked in this recipe is the tempered oil, which really ramps up what is already delicious.

Crunchy Okra

serves

4

Start by preparing the fresh okra, which is simple enough. Take the top of each okra off. Cut lengthways in half, then cut again so you have thin strips. Put in a serving dish.

Pour the oil into a small frying pan and get the oil really hot. Add the garlic and onion and fry till a deep golden colour.

Take the oil off the heat, add the chilli and ground cumin and stir through. Add the lime juice, salt and coriander and stir through again.

Pour the hot oil all over the okra, giving it all a toss so the oil gets everywhere, and it is now ready to serve.

Prep: 5 minutes

Cook: 12 minutes

280g fresh okra
100ml olive oil
4 cloves of garlic, crushed
1 onion, diced
3 red chillies, finely diced
2 teaspoons ground cumin
2 limes, juice only
large pinch of salt
small handful of fresh coriander

+ If you ever have herbs that are wilting, don't throw them out. Blitz them in the microwave in 10-second bursts to dry out and then crush and store in a jar for the next time you have a herb emergency.

Samosas are the centre of every celebration and every gathering. I love samosas and especially these ones, which we like to call shinghara. It's the over-filled, shorter cousin of the samosa. To make these from scratch is a privilege and a joy, so enjoy.

From-scratch Samosas

makes

Prep: 60 minutes (+ cooling & resting)

Cook: 60 minutes

For the filling

600g potatoes, peeled, boiled and cooled

3 tablespoons vegetable oil

3 cloves of garlic, crushed

2 onions, diced

1 teaspoon cumin

2 teaspoons salt

large handful of chopped fresh dill

For the pastry

240g plain flour

1 teaspoon salt

2 teaspoons caster sugar

4 tablespoons vegetable oil

85–90ml cold water (you may not need it all)

oil, for frying

Let's start with the filling. The potatoes need to be peeled, boiled and cooled. Pour the vegetable oil into a small frying pan and when the oil is hot, add the garlic and fry till golden.

Now add the onion, cumin and salt and cook till the onion is soft and brown.

Mash the potatoes till smooth, add the browned onion and chopped dill, mix through and leave to cool completely.

Make the pastry by putting the plain flour in a bowl with the salt, caster sugar and vegetable oil. Mix through. Slowly pour in the water, using your hands to mix all of the time. This is a really tight dough so don't be tempted to add more water to make it come together, just bring together without kneading.

As soon as your dough has come together, wrap and leave to rest for 1 hour on the worktop.

Divide the rested pastry into six equal pieces, 60g each. Roll each one out to an oval shape, about 13cm x 23cm and 2mm thin. Cut each in half so you have two semi circles.

Have water ready to seal the pastry in places. Take a semi-circle and dab water lightly across the straight edge. Pick up and fold the straight edge in half so the ends meet, sealing so you have a cone shape. Make a C shape with your index finger and thumb and place the cone in there with the flap of pastry hanging over your index finger. Fill with the potato mixture.

Lightly dab water across the outer rim of the pastry and bring the flap over to create a flat base, then seal the edges. Sit on the flat base on a lightly floured tray ready for frying.

→

Do this to all the semicircles.

Pour oil into a pan and pop on a medium heat – these need to start cooking in lukewarm oil so we get that biscuit crunch. Heat the oil to 70°C and then add your samosas. These take 30 minutes to fry, so I like to fry in batches of six.

Turn the heat up very slightly – as the oil fries you should see just a few bubbles. Turn the samosas and move every 5 minutes.

Drain on kitchen paper and eat hot. These are a labour of love but are worth every single second.

+ You don't have to make a dedicated filling to put into these samosas – ever thought about filling them with last night's, leftover curry, or the beans on toast from breakfast, or what about roast dinner? Once you have nailed the pasty you can fill it with whatever you fancy.

I crave these – they are that good. But with these, I must crave them 24 hours before I can eat them as the yellow split peas need overnight soaking. Despite so few ingredients, the lentils are transformed with simple spices and fried to perfection.

Lentil Bites

makes

25

Prep: 8 minutes (+ soaking)
Cook: 10–15 minutes

200g yellow split peas, soaked in cold water overnight
1½ teaspoons salt
3 teaspoons ground cumin
¼ teaspoon ground turmeric
3 spring onions, finely sliced
3 green chillies, finely sliced
small handful of finely sliced fresh coriander
oil, for frying

Start by taking your soaked overnight yellow split peas and draining them through a sieve or colander till they are as dry as you can get them.

Put the split peas in a blender and blend till you have a paste that isn't totally smooth and still has some bits. Transfer the mixture to a bowl, add the salt, cumin and turmeric and mix through.

Add the sliced spring onion, green chilli and coriander and mix through. Set aside to begin heating the oil.

Get the oil to 180°C. Take a heaped teaspoonful of the split peas mix and roll into a ball, gently drop into the oil and keep making balls and adding, turning and moving them occasionally and frying till they are golden on the outside.

Remove from the pan and set them to drain on some kitchen paper. Serve hot with your favourite sauce to dip them into.

+ If you don't have green chillies to hand, you can always replace with chilli flakes, cayenne or chilli powder.

I know it's easy to buy snacks, but when you make them yourself you can go the whole hog and make them spectacular. These peanuts are exactly that. Crunchy, flavourful and moreish.

Masala Peanuts

serves

Prep: 8–15 minutes

Cook: 40 minutes

- 500g peanuts
- 2 egg whites
- 1½ tablespoons salt
- 6 tablespoons art masala (see page 12)
- 30g onion granules
- 50g garlic granules

Preheat the oven to 180°C.

Find a large roasting dish or baking tray big enough to lay the nuts in one single layer. Roast the nuts till they are very lightly roasted. Leave to cool in the dish.

Whisk the egg whites till frothy and light using an electric whisk or in a freestanding mixer. Add the cooled nuts into the frothy egg whites and mix till completely coated.

Put the salt, art masala mix, onion granules and garlic granules in a small bowl and mix well. Sprinkle all over the nuts till evenly coated.

Reduce the oven temperature to 160°C.

Lay the nuts back into the dish or tray in one even layer and bake for 30 minutes, till the coating is dry.

Take the dish out and leave to cool completely. Store in an airtight jar.

+ You can freeze egg yolks and defrost them as and when you need them. I like to freeze them to brush over pastry before baking.

These potatoes are given lots of love and time to create that perfect crispiness, helped along with a generous measure of Bombay mix to add to the crunch. They are noisy in the tray and noisy in your mouth. If you like a crispy potato, you are on the right page.

Crispy, Noisy Potatoes

serves

4

Prep: 18 minutes

Cook: 60 minutes

For the potatoes

1kg baby potatoes

150ml vegetable oil

2 teaspoons fine salt, plus extra to salt the cooking water

1 lemon, juice only

3 tablespoons art masala (see page 12)

To finish

100g crispy fried onions

100g hot Bombay mix

Start with the potatoes. Put the baby potatoes in a large pan with cold water and a generous sprinkling of salt. Bring to the boil, boil for 5 minutes and then simmer for another 5. Drain the potatoes and leave to dry off a little.

Preheat the oven to 200°C and find a roasting dish big enough to fit the potatoes in an even layer.

Pour the vegetable oil into the roasting dish and pop into the oven to heat the oil up. Add the drained potatoes and toss in the oil. Using a potato masher or the base of a glass, squash the potatoes till they are flat. Sprinkle over the salt and squeeze over the juice of the whole lemon. Sprinkle on the art masala mix and toss everything around so it is evenly coated.

Bake for 50 minutes, making sure to turn the potatoes halfway.

As soon as the potatoes are crispy and brown, take the roasting dish out. Sprinkle in the crispy fried onions and lightly crush the hot Bombay mix and sprinkle that in too. Toss around the potatoes and you will have the tastiest and noisiest potatoes you have ever made or eaten.

+ Don't throw away your lemon rind – add it to a jar and top with olive oil. Leave to infuse for 2 weeks and you will have home-made lemon oil.

When I think of chutney as a Brit, I think of something that is cooked, jarred and often eaten with cheese or cold meats, but when I say chutney as a Bangladeshi, it's a very different thing altogether. Chutneys are not cooked, they are raw. Most have the same base ingredients but what makes each chutney different is the ingredient that bulks it up. I want to share with you this one basic recipe that can make you ten different chutneys.

No-need-to-wait Chutney

serves

4

Prep: 25 minutes

For the base ingredients

5 cloves of garlic, with the skin on

1 teaspoon salt

4 green chillies, finely chopped

small handful of finely chopped fresh coriander

For the main ingredients

200g blackberries

Or

4 green apples, grated, with any moisture squeezed out

Or

4 oranges, peeled and segments removed

Or

2 red onions, thinly sliced

Or

4 tomatoes, grated

Or

200g peas, boiled and cooled

Or

1 large mango, peeled and cubed

Or

4 carrots, grated

Or

2 avocados, mashed with lemon juice

Or

350g pineapple chunks, thinly sliced

This is so simple. Start with your unpeeled cloves of garlic. Thread the cloves onto a skewer, leaving a little gap between each of them. Turn on the hob to a medium flame and burn the garlic till completely black on the outside. As soon as they are all black, carefully remove and add to a pestle and mortar with the salt. Crush to a smooth paste, with the skin and all.

Scrape into a bowl and add the finely chopped green chilli and coriander.

Now, add your main ingredient – whatever that might be and whatever you fancy.

Mix with your hands to really macerate and develop the flavour. This is what makes it chutney – you can do this bit with a spoon, but it's just not the same. The chutney is now ready to eat straight away.

Now you've tried one, you have to try the other nine.

+ If you have an induction hob and no access to a gas flame, you can do a similar sort of burning technique by using a blowtorch if you have one. You can also grill the garlic till it burns the flesh – just make sure to turn it so you get it all burnt and totally black.

Fries, chips – potatoes fried in oil are one of the simplest and greatest pleasures in life. So, why not take them to a whole other level with these delicious fries? Fried and then coated with onions and chilli sauce, these are the best fries you will ever eat!

Refried Fries

serves

4–6

Prep: 8–10 minutes
Cook: 25–30 minutes

For the chilli sauce
150g ketchup
50ml water
4 green chillies
2 cloves of garlic
large handful of fresh coriander, plus extra for sprinkling
3 spring onions, sliced
good pinch of salt

For the garlic mayo
150g full-fat mayonnaise
1 clove of garlic, crushed
50ml water

For the fries
oil, for frying
2 onions, thinly sliced
salt
500g frozen fries

To serve
chopped fresh coriander
chopped chillies

So, to start this let's get going with the sauces. First the chilli sauce.

Put the ketchup in a blender with the water. Break the green chillies and add them in too. Add the cloves of garlic and tear in the coriander. Add the sliced spring onion and the salt. Blend to a smooth, delicious sauce and set aside.

Now for the garlic mayo. Put the full-fat mayonnaise, crushed garlic and water in a bowl and mix till well combined. Set aside and now on to the fries.

Take a large pan with high sides, ideal for deep-frying, and pour in the oil two-thirds of the way up. As soon as the oil gets to 180°C, add the sliced onion and cook, stirring and moving, till they are crisp and golden. As soon as they are, remove with a slotted spoon and drain on a tray lined with kitchen paper. Sprinkle with some salt.

Now fry your fries in batches till they are very crispy, again draining each batch on a tray lined with kitchen paper. You want the fries to be crispier than usual as they will be bathed in the chilli sauce.

Put the fries in a large bowl, sprinkle over the onion and toss together to mix.

Drizzle over the chilli sauce, tossing to make sure the fries are totally coated and drenched in the sauce.

Arrange the chilli fries on a large tray, drizzle over the garlic mayo, sprinkle over the chopped coriander and chillies and serve.

+ You don't have to make this with frozen fries. This recipe lends itself to using leftover chips from last night's takeaway, yesterday's roast potatoes, or even frozen potato waffles and hash browns.

If like me you love a good sandwich, then this is the recipe for you. Filled with spicy potatoes and dipped in a flavourful batter, this bread pakora is up there in the ultimate sandwich league table.

Sandwich Pakoras

makes

Prep: 35 minutes

Cook: 15 minutes

For the filling

4 medium potatoes, peeled, boiled and cooled

100g green peas, boiled and cooled

½ teaspoon salt

2 teaspoons English mustard

½ teaspoon ground turmeric

2 small green chillies, finely chopped

For the batter

300g chickpea flour, sifted

6 tablespoons cornflour

2 teaspoons chilli powder

1 teaspoon salt

water

8 slices of white bread

oil, for frying

Start with the filling. Put the peeled, boiled and cooled potatoes in a bowl and mash the mixture till you no longer have any lumps. You can do this with a ricer or potato masher.

Add the cooled peas, salt, mustard, turmeric and chopped green chilli. Mix and set aside.

Take four slices of the bread and divide the mixture among the slices, spreading the potato mixture all the way to the sides. Now add the other slices of bread on top of each one and squash down. Cut diagonally in quarters so you have four triangles, do the same with all of them and then set aside.

On to the batter. Put the chickpea flour, cornflour, chilli powder and salt in a bowl and whisk. Pour in the water and keep whisking till you have a mixture that is the consistency of double cream.

Pour enough oil into a deep frying pan to shallow-fry. Bring the oil up to a temperature of 180°C.

One by one, dip the triangles into the batter till coated and pop into the oil. Fry on both sides till golden and crispy.

Do this to all the triangles, drain on kitchen paper and you are ready to eat. I love eating these with ketchup and mayo!

+ Bread can be frozen if you ever have more than you need or are going away. Just pop your sliced bread into the freezer. You can defrost and use as normal or toast straight from frozen.

We would usually eat this using puffed rice that has either travelled a long way from Bangladesh in a suitcase or has been bought from a specialist store. That's not always an option, but that doesn't mean we have to miss out – you can use puffed rice cereal. It's a whole different texture, but it has the crunch. Mixed with onions, mustard and coriander, it's not breakfast but it is good.

Spicy Rice Puffs

serves

4

Prep: 5 minutes

Cook: 5 minutes

100g puffed rice, or puffed rice cereal

1 onion, finely diced

1 teaspoon salt

3 green chillies, chopped

large handful of chopped fresh coriander

100ml olive oil

2 teaspoons English mustard

Let's start by getting the puffed rice really crispy. Toast in a non-stick pan till golden and crisp. Take off the heat and leave to cool on a plate.

Put the onion in a bowl with the salt, chilli and coriander and mix with your hands.

Mix the olive oil and mustard in a jug till well combined. Add to the onion and mix through.

When you are ready to serve and eat, add the puffed rice, mix and eat straight away.

+ Mustard can be quite strong, so if you are looking for the same taste but milder, go for a wholegrain mustard instead.

Sweet stuff

These are classic thin pancakes, filled usually with sweet jaggery coconut, but I like to make mine with my kid's favourites – berries and peanut butter – and with their all-time favourite thing: chocolate.

Blueberry Peanut-filled Pancake Rolls

makes

12

Prep: 10 minutes (+ standing)
Cook: 20 minutes

For the batter
140g plain flour, sifted
2 medium eggs
200ml cold whole milk
100ml cold water
oil, for greasing

For the filling
200g milk chocolate, chopped
300g blueberries
300g smooth peanut butter

To serve
25g icing sugar
25g cocoa powder

Start by making the batter. Put the plain flour in a bowl, make a well in the centre and add the eggs, milk and water. Whisk to a smooth batter. Cover and leave to stand for 30 minutes.

Have the chocolate and blueberries ready and put the smooth peanut butter into a piping bag.

Brush a medium pancake pan with a small amount of oil and brush off any excess. Add 2 tablespoons of the batter into the middle of the pan and swirl till you have a thin layer.

As soon as the base just starts cooking, pipe a thin line of peanut butter onto the pancake, sprinkle over the chocolate and blueberries and encase, flapping over the two large long ends and then the short ends.

Cook all the pancakes and arrange them on a platter. Mix the icing sugar and cocoa powder and dust all over the filled pancakes.

+ You can make the pancake batter the night before and leave covered in the fridge. You can even freeze pancake batter in a zip-sealed bag.

This is my boy's absolute favourite cake – he would have it every day if I made it every day. It's a light sponge, doused in sweet fragrant milk, chilled, and then topped with simple whipped cream.

Cardamom Milk Traybake

serves

Prep: 15 minutes
Cook: 50 minutes (+ cooling)

For the cake
8 medium eggs
250g caster sugar
250g plain flour
1 lemon, zest only
1 teaspoon vanilla extract
1 teaspoon almond extract
oil, for greasing

For the sweet milk
397g tin of condensed milk
4 cardamom pods
100ml whole milk

For the top
600ml double cream
1 tablespoon icing sugar

Start by preheating the oven to 170°C and lining and greasing the base and sides of a 23cm x 33cm brownie tin.

Start on the cake by putting the eggs in a mixing bowl with the caster sugar and whisking on a high speed till the mixture triples in size, is light in colour and very fluffy. When the whisks are removed, the trail of the mixture should just sit there on top. This can take up to 10 minutes.

Sprinkle in the plain flour and fold through using a metal spoon. Add the lemon zest, vanilla and almond extracts and keep folding till you have no pockets of flour.

Pour the mixture into the tin, carefully level off and bake for 35 minutes. Take out of the oven and leave to cool in the tin.

For the sweet milk, pour the tin of condensed milk into a jug. Crush the cardamom pods, remove the husks and crush the little black seeds to a fine powder. Add to the condensed milk along with the whole milk and mix well.

Pour the milk mixture all over the cake and allow to soak through, then pop into the fridge to chill completely.

Whip up the cream with the icing sugar till you have soft peaks. Take the cake out, layer on the cream, cut into squares and serve.

If you'd like to make your traybake extra special, you can sprinkle with almond flakes, dessicated coconut or even a flourish of rose petals.

+ Any sort of cake that has dairy in it, like cream or milk, that isn't baked in should be stored in the fridge when not being eaten.

I love fried bread, so why not fried brioche? Fried bread doesn't have to always be savoury, it can be sweet and, wow, does it work, drenched in a spiced sweet milk!

Sweet Fried Brioche

makes

16

Prep: 2 minutes

Cook: 26 minutes

For the brioche

oil, for frying

8 slices of brioche, halved into triangles

For the sweet milk

600ml double cream

100ml water

1 cardamom pod, crushed

1 cinnamon stick

1 bay leaf

200g caster sugar

To serve

450g strawberries, quartered

Pour the oil into a deep frying pan and place over a medium heat.

Have a baking tray ready lined with some baking paper.

Fry all the brioche slices till they are a deep golden brown on both sides, making sure to turn and fry evenly.

For the sweet milk, pour the double cream and water into a pan with the cardamom pod, cinnamon stick and bay leaf.

Bring to the boil, reduce the heat, then add the sugar, stir in and leave to simmer.

To serve, put four triangles of the fried bread into each bowl, pour on the hot milky syrup and serve with strawberries on the side.

+ Did you know you can freeze milk and cream if you have any left over? Just freeze in the container it came in, defrost in the fridge and it's ready to use as normal.

Cheesecake is one of my favourite desserts and this version has everything a cheesecake needs: crisp, buttery filo layers, a nutty base layer and a creamy cheesecake filling with flecks of rose petal.

Badam Cheesecake

serves

10

Prep: 38 minutes

Cook: 1 hour 25 minutes (+ cooling & refrigerating)

For the filo base and sides

270g pack of filo pastry, ready-rolled

100g unsalted butter

1 teaspoon ground cinnamon

1 orange, zest only (reserve the juice)

For the nutty base

225g digestive biscuits

100g pistachios

110g unsalted butter, melted

pinch of salt

For the filling

900g full-fat cream cheese

200g caster sugar

150ml soured cream

3 tablespoons plain flour

3 medium eggs →

Start by preheating the oven to 180°C and lining and greasing the base and sides of a round 20cm loose-bottom cake tin.

Now cover the base and sides with the filo. The readymade filo sheets come in rectangles. Cut them in half so they are squares. Put the butter in a pan to melt with the cinnamon and orange zest and mix well.

Brush the inside of the tin with the cinnamon butter, lay over a sheet of the filo and brush all over with butter. Add another sheet of filo, moving clockwise as you lay the sheets so that you cover all the sides, again brushing with butter. Keep doing this till the base and sides are completely covered.

Make the nutty base by putting the digestive biscuits and pistachios in a food processor and blending to a fine, even crumb. Take out and tip into a bowl, pour in the melted butter and add the salt and mix till you have the texture of wet sand.

Tip into the prepared tin with the filo and, using the back of a spoon, press into the base in an even layer. Bake for 25 minutes, then take the tin out of the oven and set aside. Lower the oven temperature to 140°C.

Start making the filling. Put the cream cheese in a bowl with the caster sugar and mix the sugar in well. Spoon in the soured cream, plain flour and eggs and mix through. Sprinkle in your rose petals and the rose extract and mix.

Pour onto the biscuity filo base and smooth the top. Tap sharply on the worktop to remove any air pockets and sprinkle over the chopped pistachios.

Bake for 1 hour. When the hour is up, leave the oven ajar so the hot air comes out of the oven gently. Leave the cheesecake in there till the oven is cold.

1 organic rose, petals removed

½ teaspoon rose extract

100g pistachios, roughly chopped

For the syrup

juice of 1 orange

3 cardamom pods, crushed

100g caster sugar

To serve

pouring cream

rose syrup

Make the syrup by putting the orange juice in a saucepan with enough water to make up 100ml of liquid. Add the crushed cardamom pods and caster sugar. Mix it all together and then put over a high heat. As soon as the mixture boils, turn the heat down to allow the mixture to reduce to half the amount and form a thicker syrup.

Take the cheesecake out of the cold oven and drizzle the syrup around the edges into the layers of filo and on top of the nuts. Refrigerate for a minimum of 4 hours before devouring with some rose syrup and pouring cream.

+ If you don't have rose syrup, take 325g golden syrup and add a dash of pink food colouring, 1 teaspoon rose extract and 50ml cold water. Mix until combined and you now have your own home-made, vibrant rose syrup.

If my grandad was alive, I think he would have loved this. The flavours are simple: caramel-golden coconut and a soft, zesty lime cake, all in a beautiful Bundt.

Coconut Bundt Cake

serves

12

Prep: 12 minutes

Cook: 50 minutes (+ resting)

For the coconut

butter, for greasing

2–3 tablespoons plain flour, for dusting

150g desiccated coconut

2 teaspoons fennel seeds

397g tin of condensed milk

For the cake

8 medium eggs

250g soft brown sugar

2 teaspoons ground cinnamon

4 limes, zest only

250g self-raising flour, sifted

Start by greasing the inside of a 2.8-litre Bundt tin. Grease all the nooks well – more is more where this greasing is concerned. Add a few tablespoons of flour into the tin and turn the tin around so the butter catches the flour and coats the tin.

Pop the coconut into a non-stick frying pan, toast till lightly golden and put in a bowl to one side. Return the same pan to the heat and toast the fennel seeds. When aromatic, put them in a pestle and mortar and roughly grind. Pour the condensed milk into the bowl containing the coconut, then add the fennel and mix through. Pour into the base of the tin, making sure you have an even layer.

Preheat the oven to 170°C.

Make the cake by putting the eggs, soft brown sugar, cinnamon and lime zest into a large bowl and mixing till you have a mixture that is light and fluffy. Now add in the self-raising flour and mix till you have a smooth batter.

Pour in over the caramel coconut mix and bake for 45–50 minutes till a skewer inserted comes out clean.

When you take the cake out of the oven, leave it in the tin for 10 minutes and then tip out onto a serving dish. Serve while still warm.

+ Turn your leftover limes into lime ice cubes. Cut the limes into quarters, freeze and pop into your drink or coke next time. They act as ice cubes and add flavour.

This is the funnest funnel cake you will ever make! Cake batter, fried in one enormous swirl and then drenched in sweet, aromatic icing.

Funnel Cake

serves

Prep: 30 minutes

Cook: 6–8 minutes

For the batter
300g self-raising flour, sifted
½ teaspoon ground turmeric
2 tablespoons icing sugar
½ teaspoon baking powder
240ml whole milk
2 medium eggs
oil, for frying

For the icing
200g icing sugar, sifted
1 lemon, zest and juice
½ teaspoon ground cinnamon
2–4 tablespoons water

Start by making the batter. Put the self-raising flour in a bowl with the turmeric, icing sugar and baking powder and whisk together.

Make a well in the centre, pour in the milk and eggs and whisk till you have a smooth batter.

Set aside for 20 minutes and make the icing.

Put the sifted icing sugar in a bowl with the zest and juice of the lemon. Add the ground cinnamon and mix. Add tablespoons of water incrementally if needed.

Get a large non-stick 30cm frying pan. Pour in the oil to come halfway up and start heating over a medium heat.

Put the batter in a piping bag and snip off the top to make a hole the width of 1cm.

To test if the oil is hot enough, drop in a little of the batter and if it bubbles and rises to the top, it's ready to use to fry.

Now, carefully pipe, starting from the centre of the pan and moving out towards the edge in a swirly motion. Keep piping around the pan, making sure the swirls are touching and connecting, till you reach an inch of space between the cake batter and the edge of the pan. Fry gently for a few minutes till golden.

Take out very carefully and pop onto a platter. While the cake is still piping hot, drizzle and drench with the icing.

+ If you don't have icing sugar at home, just add caster sugar to a food processor with some cornflour, blend to a powder and you have readymade icing sugar.

Kulfi ice cream needs nothing else, but when you make this easy, no-churn kulfi ice cream with cardamom and then sandwich it between soft biscuits, kulfi just got better.

Kulfi Ice Cream Bars

makes

Prep: 25 minutes (+ freezing)

For the biscuit

400g custard cream biscuits

100g unsalted butter, plus extra for greasing the tin

pinch of salt

For the ice cream

4 cardamom pods

600ml double cream

200g condensed milk

2 teaspoons vanilla extract

200g raspberries, halved

100g pistachios, roughly chopped

Line and grease the base and sides of a 23cm square cake tin.

For the biscuit base and top that makes the sandwich, blitz the custard cream biscuits to a fine crumb and put in a bowl. Melt the butter and pour it in with a pinch of salt.

Take half the mixture, put in the base of the tin and spread into an even layer. Pop into the freezer and start making the ice cream.

Crush the cardamom pods, remove the husks and crush the little black seeds to a fine powder. Pour the double cream into a bowl with the condensed milk, vanilla extract and the cardamom powder and whisk till the cream comes to soft peaks.

Take the tin out of the freezer. Add in half the ice-cream mixture and sprinkle over the raspberries and pistachios. Spread the rest of the ice cream on top in an even layer, using piping to stop the fruit from moving.

Sprinkle over the rest of the biscuit mix. Leave in the freezer for at least 4 hours.

When you are ready to eat, take out for 10 minutes to soften a little, then cut into squares.

+ To stop your soft-scoop ice cream going soft and to prevent it from frosting over, always put your ice-cream tub in a zip-lock bag, seal up and pop into the freezer.

I first ate something like this in Bangladesh years ago and although it's a vague memory, I've tried to recreate what I ate. It was like a bready dough, covered in all sorts of nuts and a sticky, sweet syrup, and that is exactly what we are going to make – from memory!

Nut Bread Wheel

serves

8

Prep: 20 minutes

Cook: 20 minutes

For the dough

oil, for greasing

350g plain flour, sifted

2 tablespoons baking powder

1 teaspoon salt

170–190ml cold water

150g mixed whole roasted salted nuts, roughly chopped

For the syrup

150g golden syrup

1 orange, zest and juice

1 teaspoon ground cinnamon

Preheat the oven to 180°C and have a 30cm round baking tray/pizza tray lightly greased at the ready or a lightly greased baking tray.

Make the dough by putting the flour in a bowl with the baking powder and salt and mixing through.

Make a well in the centre, pour in the water, mix and bring the dough together.

Roll out the dough to fit your tray. Place on the tray and prick holes all over. Brush the top with water, then sprinkle over the nuts and press into the dough.

Bake in the oven for 15 minutes.

Meanwhile, make the syrup by putting the golden syrup, orange zest and juice in a small pan with the cinnamon. Mix and bring the mixture to the boil, then take off the heat.

As soon as the nut wheel comes out of the oven, cut into wedges while still hot. Pour all the syrup on top and leave it to soak it all in. Eat while still warm.

+ You could use honey, agave or maple syrup in place of the golden syrup.

Rice pudding is a staple in our home. It's as British as it is Bengali and over the years I have made so many variations. Soaking the basmati overnight gets the fermentation process going for a greater depth of flavour. This is one of my favourites, with fennel and sweet salted caramel.

Fennel caramel rice pudding

serves

8

Prep: 20 minutes (+ soaking)
Cook: 20 minutes

For the rice
150g basmati rice
500ml cold water
2½ teaspoons fennel seeds
250ml whole milk
150g caster sugar

For the caramel
200g caster sugar
125ml water
100g unsalted butter
100ml double cream
large pinch of rock salt

For the rice, start by soaking the basmati either overnight or for a minimum of 4 hours in the cold water.

Without draining it, put the rice and all the water into a blender with the fennel seeds and blend till the mixture has small grains of rice, all broken up but not a paste.

Add the rice mixture to a non-stick saucepan along with the milk and cook over medium heat till it has really thickened.

Add the sugar and cook for another 5 minutes. Transfer the mixture into individual bowls and leave to set and cool completely in the fridge.

While the rice puddings cool, make the caramel by putting the caster sugar and water in a pan. Mix and allow to come to the boil, then simmer until the mixture turns an amber colour and there are no more sugar crystals left. Add the butter and whisk through till completely melted.

Pour in the double cream and allow the mixture to come to a boil, then leave to simmer until thickened.

Take off the heat, add the salt and mix through. Take the cold rice out of the fridge and serve with the hot caramel.

+ If you haven't got cream, you can use whole milk instead to make the salted caramel. It will be thinner, but you will still have a great caramel.

This is a classic sweet dessert that we always make. It's perfect for after a meal and these stewed, almost candied, pineapples get better and better every time they get warmed up.

Stewed Pineapples

serves

6

Prep: 1–2 minutes

Cook: 46 minutes

750g frozen pineapple chunks
250g caster sugar
2 bay leaves
3 cardamom pods, crushed
1 cinnamon stick
2 teaspoons fennel seeds
150g ghee

To serve
ice cream

Put the frozen pineapple chunks in a medium non-stick pan with the caster sugar, bay leaves, cardamom pods, cinnamon and fennel seeds. Pop onto a high heat.

Let the pineapple boil in its juices for 20 minutes. Lots of liquid will be released from the pineapple. Reduce the heat and then simmer for another 20 minutes.

Add the ghee and cook gently till the pineapple has become clear and an amber colour.

Serve the stewed pineapple hot with a dollop of cold ice cream.

+ You can make this dish entirely vegan by using coconut oil instead of ghee.

Tea, biscuits and relax

Why have just a biscuit when you can have a cake that tastes like a biscuit? Sweet, crunchy and buttery.

Cake Biscuits

makes

20

Prep: 6 minutes

Cook: 1 hour 24 minutes (+ cooling)

280g readymade Madeira cake
75g ghee, melted
200g royal icing sugar
75ml cold water

Begin with your readymade Madeira cake. Cut the cake into ten equal slices, and then cut those slices in two so you have twenty pieces of cake. Lay onto a baking tray, take your melted ghee and dip each cake into the ghee till you have dipped them all. Leave them to soak it all in.

Preheat the oven to 180°C.

Bake the tray of cake for 40 minutes, making sure to turn halfway so they are crisp on both sides. Take the tray out and lower the oven temperature to 140°C fan.

Put the royal icing sugar into a bowl and add the water - you should have a mixture that is runny.

Take the tray of cake biscuits and brush with the sugar mixture till they are coated all over. Pop back into the oven and bake for 40 minutes till the sugar has dried on.

Take out and leave the biscuits to cool and then they are ready to dunk.

+ You can do this with any leftover cake or bread that is getting dry, then you have biscuits and no waste.

Chai is a love language and done well there is no going back. This spice mix packs a punch and a little goes a really long way. Whole spices, blended to give you a tea that is so aromatic and unique.

Chai

serves

8–10

Prep: 10 minutes

Cook: 15 minutes

For the chai spice blend

26g cardamom pods
13g cinnamon sticks
28g fennel seeds
8g bay leaves
35g black peppercorns
15 tea bags

For the chai

500ml whole milk
500ml water
sugar, to taste

For the chai spice blend, put the whole cardamom pods into a spice grinder or blender. Break in the cinnamon sticks as much as you can break them down – this will help grind the whole thing faster without the machine having to do much of the work. Add the fennel seeds and break in the bay leaves. Add the peppercorns and grind the spices to a fine powder.

Transfer to a bowl and add the tea leaves by cutting them out of their bags one by one. Mix and transfer the spice into a jar and label.

To make the chai, add the whole milk and water to a pan with just 1 heaped teaspoon of the spice mix. Bring the mixture to the boil and leave to simmer for 10 minutes with a lid on.

Serve the chai in the smallest glasses or cups you can find. I like to use Turkish teacups or espresso cups. Add sugar to the base of each cup. Yes, chai should be drunk sweet, but you can add as little or as much as you would like. Pour in the chai through a small tea sieve to remove the grainy lumps, stir and drink.

+ Use this chai blend to spice up your bakes, flapjacks, Christmas cake or carrot cake. It's so versatile but, remember, a little goes a long way.

We only ever ate condensed milk when we needed something sweet after eating curry. We would eat hot rice and condensed milk and, wow, what a combination. But I wanted to make a sweet treat using condensed milk that was a little more than just pouring it out of a tin. These are simply sweet and moreish.

Condensed Milk Cookies

makes

12

Prep: 20 minutes (+ chilling)

Cook: 12–15 minutes

30g desiccated coconut

150g unsalted butter, softened, plus extra for greasing the trays

150g caster sugar

200ml condensed milk

300g self-raising flour, sifted

Start by toasting the desiccated coconut in a non-stick pan over a medium to high heat. Keep stirring and moving the coconut so it doesn't catch. As soon as the coconut is golden, take off the heat, remove from the pan and leave to cool.

Add the unsalted butter to a bowl with the caster sugar and whisk till the mixture is light and fluffy. Pour in the condensed milk and whisk till you have runnier mixture.

Now, pour in the flour and cooled coconut and mix with a spoon till you have a thick dough mixture. Divide the mixture into 12 equal balls and pop on a tray to chill in the fridge for 30 minutes.

Preheat the oven to 160°C. Line and lightly grease two baking trays.

Pop the dough balls on the trays, spaced out from each other to give them room to spread. Push down on them very lightly to flatten a little.

Bake for 12–15 minutes, till a very light golden brown. Take out and leave to cool completely on the tray. When they are cool, they are ready to eat.

+ These can be cooked from frozen if you want to make the dough in advance. Simply pop on a tray and bake for 20 minutes.

I grew up drinking hot sweet tea that was simmered so long it took on the texture of cream. Cold tea is a thing I only tried when I was old enough to buy my own drinks and even when I did, the idea was unnerving. However, I do like an iced tea, so I've merged the worlds and come up with a delicious sweet tea that is light with oat milk and bursting with bay flavour.

Iced Caramel Bay Tea

serves

Cook: 25 minutes (+ cooling)

For the milk tea
1 litre oat milk
6 bay leaves
4 tea bags

For the caramel
200g caster sugar
pinch of salt
60ml water

To serve
ice
golden syrup
pinch of salt

Begin by pouring the oat milk into a large pan with the bay leaves and tea bags. Bring the mixture to the boil and simmer for 5 minutes, then turn off and leave the bay to infuse. Take off the heat and start on the caramel.

Put the caster sugar in a small pan with the pinch of salt and water. Mix the water and sugar, pop onto a medium heat and allow the sugar to melt. You will start to see the colour get brown around the edges. Mix and keep it on the same heat, allowing the mixture to go a golden brown.

As soon as it's golden brown and the sugar has dissolved, pour in two ladlefuls of the hot milk tea from the pan and allow the caramel to mix into it. It may spit a little so be sure to stand back or just be aware. Bring to the boil and let it bubble, allowing the caramel to mix in with the milk.

Now pour the caramel milk mixture into the big pan of milk tea and stir till well combined. Take off the heat and leave to cool. Remove the tea bags, leave the bay leaves in and chill completely.

To serve, drizzle golden syrup into the inside of the glasses or dip the rim of the glasses into syrup and then coat with salt. Do either or do both.

Fill the glass with ice and pour in the cooled milk.

+ If you have any iced milk left over but not enough to make a full drink, don't pour it down the sink. Pop into ice cube trays and freeze and you will have iced tea cubes to add extra flavour to your iced tea next time.

This includes two of my favourite things and I have made their worlds collide: flapjack – sticky, sweet and oaty – topped with a spiced Indian milk fudge. Why have one world when you can build a bridge between two.

Milk Fudge Flapjack

makes

12

Prep: 12 minutes

Cook: 45 minutes (+ chilling)

For the flapjack

250g unsalted butter, plus extra for greasing the tin

180g golden syrup

180g caster sugar

500g porridge oats

2 teaspoons almond extract

For the milk fudge

60g unsalted butter

200ml double cream

60g caster sugar

6 cardamom pods

100ml condensed milk

250g semi-skimmed milk powder, blitzed in a processor to remove any lumps

100g toasted almond flakes

For the flapjack, start by putting the butter, golden syrup and caster sugar into a pan and warming it all through till the butter has melted and sugar dissolved. Take off the heat.

Preheat the oven to 160°C fan and line and grease the base and sides of a 20cm square cake tin.

Add the oats to a bowl, pour in the melted butter/sugar mix and add the almond extract. Stir the mixture till everything is well combined.

Tip into the prepared tin and flatten into the tin making sure to pat down so everything is well compressed.

Pop into the oven and bake for 30 minutes. When the flapjack is ready, it will be golden around the edges and lighter in the centre. Take out and leave to cool completely, then chill in the fridge so we have a firm base for our fudge to sit on.

For the milk fudge, put the unsalted butter, double cream and caster sugar into a pan and mix till the sugar has dissolved.

Crush the cardamom pods, remove the husks and crush the black seeds. Add to the sugar mix. Stir in and then add the condensed milk and semi-skimmed milk powder. Bring to a gentle simmer over a medium heat and keep stirring till the mixture is thick and coming away from the sides of the pan.

Spoon the mixture right on top of the flapjack and press into an even layer. Sprinkle over the toasted almond flakes and press them in.

Leave to cool in the tin and then leave to chill in the fridge. Cut into squares and they are ready.

+ If you wanted, you could make the two parts of this recipe completely separately and serve them as two entirely different recipes. It's not bad when you get two recipes for one!

We grew up drinking buffalo milk, unpasteurised and warm from the buffalo itself. So, nut milks were not a thing I had ever thought about until I began considering the environment and the benefits of trying alternative milks. Nut milks need not be boring or out of a carton. They are easy to make and I must share my pistachio milk with you – it's delicious.

Pistachio Milk

makes about 1 litre

Prep: 20 minutes
(+ soaking & chilling)

250g pistachios
1 teaspoon fennel seeds
1 litre cold water
½ vanilla pod
sugar, honey or maple syrup, to sweeten (optional)

Start by roasting the pistachios – this will really help to bring out their flavour and colour. Roast the nuts till they are golden and you can smell the nutty aroma in the air.

Put the nuts in a bowl with hot water, submerging till the nuts are just covered. Add the fennel seeds, mix through and leave to soak for 1 hour.

Drain the soaking water and add the pistachios and fennel seeds to a blender. Blend to a rough paste. Now add the cold water along with the seeds of the vanilla pod and blend till smooth.

I like to leave the milk in a jug to sit and chill in the fridge for 1 hour to really extract the milky goodness.

Strain the milk and decant it into a glass bottle. You can sweeten this using sugar, honey or maple syrup, if desired. Drink iced or use in your smoothies.

+ Don't get rid of the pulp left in the sieve after straining. You can use it in smoothies or drain out any more excess liquid and use it in a cookie batter mixture to add a nutty texture and flavour.

Quinoa isn't a grain that I grew up eating, but we did puffed rice with tea a lot and this kind of reminds me of that. I just love this treat a little bit more because of the miniature pops all surrounded in chocolate.

Popped Quinoa Shards

makes

1

Prep: 10 minutes
Cook: 10-12 minutes (+ cooling)

200g quinoa
225g dark chocolate
½ teaspoon ground cinnamon
225g white chocolate

Let's start with the fun job of popping the quinoa. Take a medium non-stick pan and put over a high heat. As soon as the pan is hot, reduce the heat to medium and add a quarter of the quinoa in a thin layer across the pan bottom. Move the pan around occasionally to move the quinoa – you should start to hear popping and the quinoa will begin to get puffy. Keep on doing this till all the quinoa has popped.

Transfer to a bowl and repeat with the rest of the quinoa in batches till you have done all of it.

Have a large baking tray ready lined with some baking paper.

Melt the dark chocolate in a bowl (either over a pan of simmering water or in the microwave in 30-second bursts on low, stirring in between), and add the ground cinnamon. Melt the white chocolate in a separate bowl. The chocolates now need to be cooled – if the popped quinoa is added to warm chocolate it will lose its crunch.

Divide the quinoa equally into the two bowls and mix through. Dollop alternately onto the tray and spread using a spatula, then leave the mixture to set fast in the fridge.

Take the sheet out when you are ready to serve and simply break into shards and eat.

+ These shards make a great decoration for the sides and tops of cakes. So, if you are making something special, this is a lovely home-made decoration to try out.

These are one of my favourite biscuits to eat. Crisp, buttery and, best of all, fried so they take on a whole other flavour. The outer layer is crisp and the inner slightly softer. It's the biscuit that keeps on giving and giving – and that is my kind of biscuit.

Powdered Nimki Biscuits

makes

10

Prep: 20 minutes

Cook: 15 minutes

For the dough

250g plain flour, sifted, plus a little extra for dusting

1 teaspoon salt

3 teaspoons fennel seeds, crushed

100g ghee, softened

100ml cold water

vegetable oil, for frying

For the spread

25g plain flour

25g ghee, softened

50g pistachios, crushed to a powder

To serve

icing sugar

For the dough, start by putting the plain flour in a bowl with the salt and crushed fennel seeds. Mix well and add the softened ghee.

Using your fingertips, rub in the ghee till there are no more large lumps. Drizzle in the cold water and, using your hands, bring the dough together. Roll the dough out to a 30cm x 15cm rectangle.

Make the spread by adding the plain flour and softened ghee to a bowl and mixing to a smooth paste. Spread all over the rectangle, then sprinkle on the crushed pistachio powder.

Roll the rectangle from the longer side up to create a long sausage shape with a swirl of the nut mix in the middle. Now cut into ten equal pieces. Pop the pieces onto a tray and prepare to start frying.

Have a tray ready with some kitchen paper to drain off any excess oil.

Put the oil in a medium saucepan with enough oil to go two-thirds of the way up. Put over a high heat till the oil reaches 180°C, then lower the heat.

On a lightly floured surface, roll out the dough into 10cm circles. Fold in half into a semicircle, then in half again. Now simply pinch the two corners of the curved part of the triangle. Do this to all of them and pop them onto a tray.

Fry the biscuits slowly, a few at a time, over a medium to low heat to cook through the inside layers as well as the outer layers. Do this to all the triangles and leave to drain on the kitchen paper.

Have the icing sugar ready in a bowl. While the biscuits are still warm, toss them around in plenty of icing sugar. When they have cooled completely, toss them in some more icing sugar till they are covered again.

Then they are ready to devour!

+ You can make these vegan by using coconut oil instead of ghee or butter, so why not give it a go.

Having 'pound biscuits' in Bangladesh was a real treat – you only ever ate them if guests brought them over. They were very simple butter biscuits, sometimes decorated with a little colour. They were never filled though, so I thought why not? This is my version: buttery, cinnamon biscuit wedges filled with a sweet surprise.

Sweet Filled Shortbread Wedges

makes

6

Prep: 32 minutes (+ freezing)
Cook: 50 minutes

For the shortbread
120g rice flour
250g unsalted butter, softened, plus extra for greasing the tin
120g caster sugar
250g plain flour, sifted
2 teaspoons ground cinnamon

For the filling
100g cottage cheese
4 cardamom pods
1 teaspoon fennel seeds
1 tablespoon plain flour
50g caster sugar

To serve
icing sugar

Start with the shortbread. Add the rice flour to a non-stick frying pan and put it onto the hob on a medium to high heat. Keep stirring till the rice is golden brown. Take off the heat and leave to cool completely.

Put the softened unsalted butter in a large bowl with the caster sugar and mix till you have mixture that is smooth and creamy. This can take up to 5 minutes.

Now add the plain flour, toasted rice flour and ground cinnamon and mix till you have a dough. Flatten the dough to an even round and cut right in half. Take one half, flatten some more, then wrap in baking paper and leave in the freezer for at least 1 hour.

Grease the inside and line a round 20-cm loose-bottom cake tin.

Take the remaining shortbread mixture and press into the tin in an even layer, making sure to create a very small 5mm lip around the edge so the filling doesn't run over. Pop into the freezer while you make the filling.

For the filling, put the cottage cheese in a bowl. Crush the cardamom pods, remove the green outer husk and crush the black seeds to a fine powder along with the fennel seeds. Add to the cottage cheese with the plain flour and caster sugar.

Take the shortbread base out of the freezer. Spoon in the filling, right up to the raised lip, and spread evenly. Leave in the fridge to chill.

When the other half of the pastry has had at least 1 hour in the freezer, take it out. Grate on top of the sweet filling till you have no more dough left. Pop the tart back into the fridge.

→

Preheat the oven to 170°C.

When you are ready to bake, take the shortbread out of the fridge, sprinkle with icing sugar and bake for 45-50 minutes till golden brown.

As soon as it comes out of the oven, score using a sharp knife into six equal wedges and leave to cool in the tin. Take out and they are ready to serve, dusted with icing sugar to finish.

+ Shortbread can make a great alternative to pastry. Use it in the same way and you get a rich, decadent pastry for tarts and pies.

We grew up eating these puff pastry rectangles. Light and sweet, they came stacked in a packet, crispy with a layer of shiny sugar on top. Here I am creating my own, using rough puff pastry for the buttery layers and creating that same sweet, crunchy top.

Sugar Puffs

makes

16

Prep: 32 minutes (+ chilling)

Cook: 50 minutes

For the rough puff pastry

250g strong bread flour, plus extra for dusting

1 teaspoon fine salt

250g butter, cubed and chilled

100ml cold water (you may need more)

For the glaze

1 whole egg

1 egg yolk

120g caster sugar

We need to start by making the rough puff pastry as this is the longest part of the recipe. Put the strong bread flour into a large bowl with the fine salt and mix it together. Add the butter and mix through so the cubes are coated in the flour. Now gently rub the butter in without breaking up the pieces too much. Some will rub in more than others.

Make a well in the centre, pour in the cold water and bring the dough together. If you have too many dry patches of flour, add a few more tablespoons at a time till you have a dough that has fully come together.

Tip the dough out onto a floured surface and then gently bring the dough together without kneading. Shape into a rectangle and flatten the dough. Wrap in clingfilm and leave to chill in the fridge for 1 hour.

After it has chilled, take out the dough, unwrap and roll out on a floured surface to a 20cm x 50cm rectangle.

Fold one third of the dough into the middle third and then fold the other third over, so you have three layers if you look at it from the side.

Give it a quarter turn, roll again to a rectangle and fold again - one third into the middle third and then the other third over. Cover, wrap and pop into the fridge for 1 hour.

Preheat the oven to 200°C. Have two baking trays ready, and with two sheets of baking paper big enough to fit the trays.

Roll out the pastry to a 30cm x 20cm rectangle. Put a sheet of paper on a baking tray. Place the pastry on top.

Cut down the middle across the length and then cut vertically

→

across eight times so you have 16 rectangles. Poke holes into each rectangle to create pockets for steam to escape. Put another sheet of baking paper on top. Put another tray on top to weigh it down and bake like this for 45 minutes.

Take out of the oven and carefully remove the top tray and sheet of paper. Using a sharp knife, carefully cut through the pastry to create individual bars.

Now make the glaze by putting the egg, egg yolk and caster sugar into a bowl. Whisk the mixture till well combined.

Brush the bars all over with the egg mix, making sure to get the edges and sides, and pop back in the oven. Keep an eye on them this time and leave them in there for just enough time to create a golden, shiny crust.

Take out and leave to cool completely on the tray. They are now ready to be eaten, dipped or even served with ice cream.

+ You could cheat – you don't have to make your own pastry. This will work just as well if you use shop-bought puff pastry.

INDEX

A

almonds: frangipane almond parathas 24-5
  Peshwari naans 78
aloo burgers 40
anchovies: smoky aubergine pizza 146-9
apples: no-need-to-wait chutney 176
art masala 12
  beef lemon balti 113
  chicken liver grills 46
  chicken rolls 160
  chicken wings 42
  crispy leek biryani 66-7
  crispy, noisy potatoes 174
  keema plate pie 95-7
  lamb kebabs 57
  masala fries 136
  masala peanuts 173
  rocking roast chicken 58
  saag aloo chicken jalfrezi 101
  whole baked cauliflower 150-1
  yoghurt chicken 88
aubergines: smoky aubergine pizza 146-9
avocados: no-need-to-wait chutney 176

B

back-of-the-fridge pakoras 154
badam cheesecake 192-3
Bangladeshi breakfast loaf 18-20
bay leaves 10
  brown daal 123
  chai 211
  chicken korma 114
  crispy leek biryani 66-7
  duck and cabbage 109
  duck egg bhuna 102
  iced caramel bay tea 214
  pulao 82
  roasted toasted oats 33
  stewed pineapples 204
  sweet fried brioche 190
  vermicelli slices 37
beef: beef lemon balti 113
  dhansak bake 110
  kati rolls 53
biryani, crispy leek 66-7
biscuits: badam cheesecake 192-3
  cake biscuits 208
  condensed milk cookies 212
  kulfi ice cream bars 199
  powdered nimki biscuits 222
blackberries: no-need-to-wait chutney 176
blueberry peanut-filled pancake rolls 186
Bombay potatoes 120
bread: Bangladeshi breakfast loaf 18-20
  chocolate bread pudding 23
  dinner rolls 69
  frangipane almond parathas 24-5
  freezing 20, 23
  green pea parathas 72
  kati rolls 53
  lacy rotis 74
  paneer and chilli loaf 77
  Peshwari naans 78
  pooris 80
  rice rotis 85
  sandwich pakoras 181
  sweet fried brioche 190
brioche: sweet fried brioche 190
brown daal 123
burgers: aloo burgers 40
burrata: smoky aubergine pizza 146-9
butter beans: keema plate pie 95-7

C

cabbage: duck and cabbage 109
  rocking roast chicken 58
cake biscuits 208
cakes and bakes: badam cheesecake 192-3

cake biscuits 208
cardamom milk traybake 189
coconut bundt cake 194
funnel cake 197
milk fudge flapjack 217
nut bread wheel 200
sugar puffs 227-9
sweet filled shortbread wedges 224-6
sweet fried brioche 190
vermicelli slices 37
caramel: fennel caramel rice pudding 203
cardamom 10
art masala 12
badam cheesecake 192-3
cardamom milk traybake 189
chai 211
chicken korma 114
crispy leek biryani 66-7
duck and cabbage 109
kulfi ice cream bars 199
milk fudge flapjack 217
mint grapes with yoghurt 30
pulao 82
stewed pineapples 204
sweet filled shortbread wedges 224-6
sweet fried brioche 190
vermicelli slices 37
carrots: lamb kebabs 57
no-need-to-wait chutney 176
rocking roast chicken 58
cashew nuts: charred mango salad 124
Peshwari naans 78
cauliflower: whole baked cauliflower 150-1
cavolo nero: greens 135
chai 211
cheese: cheesy kachori 156
courgette paneer pasta 129
dhansak bake 110
freezing 156
paneer and chilli loaf 77
smoky aubergine pizza 146-9
cheesecake, badam 192-3
chicken: as alternative ingredient 26
chicken korma 114
chicken rolls 160
chicken wings 42

rocking roast chicken 58
saag aloo chicken jalfrezi 101
stock 59
yoghurt chicken 88
chicken liver grills 46
chilli powder 11
art masala 12
charred mango salad 124
cheesy kachori 156
citrus tiger prawns 106
courgette paneer pasta 129
duck and cabbage 109
duck egg bhuna 102
egg fried rice 49
masala fries 136
paneer and chilli loaf 77
rice basket eggs 145
seafood kofta curry 98
smoky aubergine pizza 146-9
spicy salmon and onions 61
tangy tomato prawns 62
velvet eggs on toast 34
watermelon rind curry 130
whole salmon masala 90-3
chillies: aloo burgers 40
back-of-the-fridge pakoras 154
brown daal 123
crab bhuna 105
crispy fried noodles 45
crispy leek biryani 66-7
crunchy okra 162
egg fried rice 49
green mackerel salad 50
greens 135
lentil bites 170
no-need-to-wait chutney 176
raw yellow lentil salad 142
refried fries 178-9
revival fish broth 54
saag aloo chicken jalfrezi 101
sandwich pakoras 181
spicy rice puffs 182
spicy salmon and onions 61
watermelon rind curry 130
yoghurt chicken 88
chocolate: chocolate bread pudding 23
popped quinoa shards 221
chutney, no-need-to-wait 176
cinnamon 11
art masala 12
badam cheesecake 192-3
chai 211
chicken korma 114
crispy leek biryani 66-7
dhansak bake 110
duck and cabbage 109
frangipane almond parathas 24-5
funnel cake 197
mint grapes with yoghurt 30
nut bread wheel 200
popped quinoa shards 221
pulao 82
stewed pineapples 204
sweet filled shortbread wedges 224-6
sweet fried brioche 190
vermicelli slices 37
watermelon rind curry 130
clementines: citrus tiger prawns 106
cocoa powder: blueberry peanut-filled pancake rolls 186
chocolate bread pudding 23
coconut cream: watermelon rind curry 130
coconut, desiccated: coconut bundt cake 194
condensed milk cookies 212
Peshwari naans 78
watermelon rind curry 130
coconut milk: roasted toasted oats 33
condensed milk: cardamom milk traybake 189
coconut bundt cake 194
condensed milk cookies 212
kulfi ice cream bars 199
milk fudge flapjack 217
cookies: condensed milk cookies 212
cottage cheese: sweet filled shortbread wedges 224-6
courgettes: courgette paneer pasta 129
revival fish broth 54
crab bhuna 105
cream: caramel fennel rice pudding 203
cardamom milk traybake 189
kulfi ice cream bars 199

milk fudge flapjack 217
sweet fried brioche 190
vermicelli slices 37
cream cheese: badam cheesecake 192-3
crispy fried noodles 45
cumin 11
aloo burgers 40
art masala 12
brown daal 123
charred mango salad 124
cheesy kachori 156
courgette paneer pasta 129
crunchy okra 162
duck and cabbage 109
lentil bites 170
paneer and chilli loaf 77
smoky aubergine pizza 146-9
velvet eggs on toast 34
watermelon rind curry 130
curry powder 11
art masala 12
crab bhuna 105
crispy fried noodles 45
dhansak bake 110
duck and cabbage 109
duck egg bhuna 102
egg fried rice 49
green pea parathas 72
hash smash breakfast 29
kati rolls 53
masala fries 136
seafood kofta curry 98
watermelon rind curry 130

D

daal: brown daal 123
dates: ginger butter rice 26
dhansak bake 110
dinner rolls 69
drinks: chai 211
iced caramel bay tea 214
pistachio milk 218
duck and cabbage 109
duck egg bhuna 102

E

eggs: crispy fried noodles 45
crispy leek biryani 66-7
dhansak bake 110
duck egg bhuna 102
egg fried rice 49
freezing egg yolks 173
hash smash breakfast 29
rice basket eggs 145
velvet eggs on toast 34
eight-spice mix 12

F

fennel seeds 10-11
art masala 12
chai 211
chocolate bread pudding 23
fennel caramel rice pudding 203
pistachio milk 218
powdered nimki biscuits 222
stewed pineapples 204
sweet filled shortbread wedges 224-6
fish: green mackerel salad 50
revival fish broth 54
seafood kofta curry 98
spicy salmon and onions 61
whole salmon masala 90-3
frangipane almond parathas 24-5
freezer use: bread 20, 23
cheese 156
chicken 42
drinks 216
egg yolks 173
kebabs 57
milk and cream 190
nuts 30
onions 67
parathas 25
from-scratch-samosas 164-9
funnel cake 197

G

garlic: Bombay potatoes 120
brown daal 123
chicken korma 114
garlic granules 135

garlic paste 160
greens 135
no-need-to-wait chutney 176
okra saalom 139
refried fries 178-9

gelato: watermelon 130

ghee rice 70

ginger: beef lemon balti 113
chicken korma 114
chicken liver grills 46
duck and cabbage 109
ginger butter rice 26
pulao 82
raw yellow lentil salad 142
rocking roast chicken 58
watermelon rind curry 130
yoghurt chicken 88

grapes: mint grapes with yoghurt 30

green beans: crab bhuna 105

green pea parathas 72

greens 135

H

hash smash breakfast 29

herbs: drying out 162

I

ice cream: kulfi ice cream bars 199

iced caramel bay tea 214

K

kachori, cheesy 156

kale: green mackerel salad 50
greens 135

kati rolls 53

kebabs: lamb 57

keema plate pie 95-7

kulfi ice cream bars 199

L

lacy rotis 74

lamb: keema plate pie 95-7
lamb kebabs 57

leeks: crispy leek biryani 66-7

lemons: beef lemon balti 113
crispy, noisy potatoes 174
egg fried rice 49
fridge freshener 49
funnel cake 197
green mackerel salad 50
okra saalom 139
raw yellow lentil salad 142
tangy tomato prawns 62
whole baked cauliflower 150-1

lentils: brown daal 123
dhansak bake 110
lentil bites 170
raw yellow lentil salad 142

lime pickle: brown daal 123

limes: coconut bundt cake 194
courgette paneer pasta 129
crunchy okra 162
mint grapes with yoghurt 30

linseeds: ginger butter rice 26

liver: chicken liver grills 46

M

mackerel: green mackerel salad 50

mangetout: revival fish broth 54
mango: charred mango salad 124
  no-need-to-wait chutney 176
maple syrup: ginger butter rice 26
masala fries 136
masala peanuts 173
milk fudge flapjack 217
milk powder: milk fudge flapjack 217
mint: lamb kebabs 57
  mint grapes with yoghurt 30
mustard: kati rolls 53
  sandwich pakoras 181
  spicy rice puffs 182

N

naans, Peshwari 78
no-need-to-wait chutney 176
noodles: crispy fried noodles 45
  vermicelli slices 37
nut bread wheel 200
nuts: storage 30

O

oats: milk fudge flapjack 217
  roasted toasted oats 33
oil: leftover usage 136
  smell removal 53
okra: crunchy okra 162
  okra saalom 139
onions: back-of-the-fridge pakoras 154
  beef lemon balti 113
  Bombay potatoes 120
  brown daal 123
  charred mango salad 124
  chicken korma 114
  chicken liver grills 46
  chicken rolls 160
  citrus tiger prawns 106
  crab bhuna 105
  crispy fried noodles 45
  crispy, noisy potatoes 174
  crunchy okra 162
  dhansak bake 110
  duck and cabbage 109
  duck egg bhuna 102
  egg fried rice 49
  green mackerel salad 50
  greens 135
  kati rolls 53
  lamb kebabs 57
  no-need-to-wait chutney 176
  okra saalom 139
  paneer and chilli loaf 77
  pulao 82
  raw yellow lentil salad 142
  refried fries 178-9
  revival fish broth 54
  rocking roast chicken 58
  saag aloo chicken jalfrezi 101
  from-scratch-samosas 164-9
  seafood kofta curry 98
  spicy rice puffs 182
  spicy salmon and onions 61
  watermelon rind curry 130
  whole baked cauliflower 150-1
  yoghurt chicken 88
oranges: badam cheesecake 192-3
  no-need-to-wait chutney 176
  nut bread wheel 200

P

pakoras: sandwich pakoras 181
pakoras, back-of-the-fridge 154
pancake rolls, blueberry peanut-filled 186
paneer: courgette paneer pasta 129
  paneer and chilli loaf 77
parathas: alternative fillings 34
  frangipane almond 24-5
  green pea 72
pasta: courgette paneer pasta 129
pastry leftovers 97
peanut butter: blueberry peanut-filled pancake rolls 186
peanuts: masala peanuts 173
peas: green pea parathas 72
  no-need-to-wait chutney 176
  sandwich pakoras 181
pecans: mint grapes with yoghurt 30
peppers: crab bhuna 105
  okra saalom 139
  saag aloo chicken jalfrezi 101
Peshwari naans 78

pies: keema plate pie 95-7
pine nuts: courgette paneer pasta 129
pineapple: no-need-to-wait chutney 176
  stewed pineapples 204
pistachios: badam cheesecake 192-3
  kulfi ice cream bars 199
  pistachio milk 218
  powdered nimki biscuits 222
  whole baked cauliflower 150-1
pizza: smoky aubergine 146-9
pooris 80
popped quinoa shards 221
potatoes: aloo burgers 40
  Bombay potatoes 120
  crispy, noisy potatoes 174
  dhansak bake 110
  hash smash breakfast 29
  lamb kebabs 57
  masala fries 136
  refried fries 178-9
  saag aloo chicken jalfrezi 101
  sandwich pakoras 181
  from-scratch-samosas 164-9
powdered nimki biscuits 222
prawns: citrus tiger prawns 106
  revival fish broth 54
  tangy tomato prawns 62
pulao 82

Q

quinoa: popped quinoa shards 221

R

raisins: Peshwari naans 78
raspberries: kulfi ice cream bars 199
refried fries 178-9
revival fish broth 54
rice: basic cooking method 15
  charred mango salad 124
  crispy leek biryani 66-7
  egg fried rice 49
  fennel caramel rice pudding 203
  ghee rice 70
  ginger butter rice 26
  pulao 82
  spicy rice puffs 182
rice flour/ground rice: rice rotis 85
rice paper: rice basket eggs 145
roses: badam cheesecake 192-3
rotis: lacy rotis 74
  rice rotis 85

S

salads: charred mango salad 124
  crunchy okra 162
  green mackerel salad 50
  raw yellow lentil salad 142
salmon: spicy salmon and onions 61
  whole salmon masala 90-3
samosas: from-scratch 164-9
sandwich pakoras 181
seafood: citrus tiger prawns 106
  crab bhuna 105
  revival fish broth 54
  seafood kofta curry 98
  tangy tomato prawns 62
shortbread: sweet filled shortbread wedges 224-6
smoky aubergine pizza 146-9
soup: revival fish broth 54
sour cream: badam cheesecake 192-3
spices: art masala 12
  overview 8-11
  rejuvenating 13
spinach: green mackerel salad 50
  greens 135
  revival fish broth 54
  saag aloo chicken jalfrezi 101
spring onions: aloo burgers 40
  back-of-the-fridge pakoras 154
  hash smash breakfast 29
  keema plate pie 95-7
  lentil bites 170
  refried fries 178-9
  rice basket eggs 145
sugar puffs 227-9
sweet fried brioche 190

T

tamarind paste/sauce: Bombay potatoes 120
  tangy tomato prawns 62
tea: chai 211
  iced caramel bay tea 214

tomato soup: saag aloo chicken jalfrezi 101
tomatoes: no-need-to-wait chutney 176
seafood kofta curry 98
tangy tomato prawns 62
whole salmon masala 90-3
tortilla wraps: as alternative ingredient 145
kati rolls 53
turmeric
Bangladeshi breakfast loaf 18-20
Bombay potatoes 120
brown daal 123
citrus tiger prawns 106
crab bhuna 105
crispy fried noodles 45
duck and cabbage 109
duck egg bhuna 102
funnel cake 197
lentil bites 170
rocking roast chicken 58
sandwich pakoras 181
seafood kofta curry 98
spicy salmon and onions 61
tangy tomato prawns 62
watermelon rind curry 130
whole baked cauliflower 150-1
whole salmon masala 90-3

V

vegetables see also specific vegetables:
back-of-the-fridge pakoras 154
pulao 82
velvet eggs on toast 34
vermicelli slices 37

W

watermelon rind curry 130

Y

yoghurt: lamb kebabs 57
mint grapes with yoghurt 30
Peshwari naans 78
yoghurt chicken 88

THANKS

Firstly, I want to say a blanket thank you to every single person who has helped to make this book happen. By everyone, I mean the delivery drivers who know to quietly knock on the door when I have my ingredients delivered at 6 a.m., so I can attempt do things quietly, but know, very well, that the smell of cooking WILL wake them up!

Testing recipes is where it all starts, so thank you to Georgia May for testing alongside me, for eating and cooking on repeat for me.

Chris Terry, the best guy ever, I would quite literally not be able to stand in front of that camera if he was not behind it. Thank you for always believing in me, my food and face.

Thank you to Rob Allison, Holly Cochrane and Luke Boatwright, for running around like headless chickens and still knowing how to cook an actual chicken! You guys are the best.

Sarah Fraser, now I know when you do that sudden pause and take a moment to think before you answer, it's because you had this in mind. Thank you for always seeing my vision and making it what it is.

Heather B, where would I be without you? Puffy-eyed, dishevelled in a creased headscarf, no doubt. Thank you for making work feel, well, not like work. May we laugh together forever.

Anne, my main lady, she does way more for me than most. A thank you in the book doesn't do it justice, but thank you all the same.

Thank you to Dan and Dan. From my dining table sat in the conservatory, eating seconds, to the book in our hands. Thank you so much for believing in me and the book.

To the entire MJ team, Gaby, Ciara, Vicky, Aggie, Bea, Dan PB and Kay, thank you for being a part of yet another big project - none of this would have come off the ground without you guys.

Abdal, Musa, Dawud and Maryam, now you have all the recipes in writing, get cooking!

Nadiya
x

michael joseph

UK | USA | Canada | Ireland | Australia
India | New Zealand | South Africa

Michael Joseph is part of the Penguin Random House group of companies whose addresses can be found at global.penguinrandomhouse.com.

First published in Great Britain by Michael Joseph, 2023
003

All oven temperatures are fan unless otherwise specified.

Set in Clever, Macklin and Eksell Display

Colour reproduction by Altaimage Ltd
Printed in Italy by Printer Trento Ltd S.r.L.

A CIP catalogue record for this book is available from the British Library

ISBN: 978-0-241-62000-7

www.greenpenguin.co.uk